+2

Sometimes on Saturday

Pearl Murray

Stronach Media Ltd

Published by **Stronach Media Ltd.**
Tullynessle, Alford, Aberdeenshire AB33 8QN

© Pearl Murray
ISBN 1 897672 03 9

First edition : September, 1994

Designed and typeset by Stronach Media Ltd.

Printed in Scotland by BPC-AUP, Aberdeen.

Cover artwork by Susan Bell.

ACKNOWLEDGEMENTS

I am grateful to my friends Shirley Cunningham, for her constant encouragement, and Judith Paris, whose idea this book was. I am also indebted to my colleague and friend Norman Harper, of Stronach Media Ltd., whose generous help has been much needed and greatly appreciated.
I would like, too, to acknowledge Aberdeen Journals Ltd., for their permission to reproduce the photographs on Pages 25, 51

For my brother
Kenneth
with much love

THE AUTHOR

A RECTOR of Fraserburgh Academy, the late Mr W.D. Kennedy, once publicly described his former pupil Pearl Murray as an outstanding student of English and "probably the best essay-writer the school has ever had".

Throughout a distinguished journalistic career, she proved the compliment well-founded. Her writing carried always the stamp of quality and was often infused by deeply felt social concern. Her pen was never more eloquent than when championing the rights of disadvantaged people, whoever they were.

At a time when the Fourth Estate was falling perceptibly in public esteem, she stood out as an exemplary exponent, a journalist of warmth, compassion and complete integrity.

She won an enviable popularity and became a much-respected public figure in her native North-east, where she chose to live and work, forfeiting, in so doing, a career on national newspapers.

By the time she gave up full-time work, in 1987, her reputation as a writer was established well beyond the North-east. In fact, her freelance columns contributed after that served to make her name better known than ever.

This book is a selection of some of her weekend pieces which appeared regularly on Saturdays. They reflect many facets of life, sometimes humorously, sometimes poignantly. From trysting with a fox to wartime memories of the North-east; from graduations to canine beauty queens; the common humanity of celebrating the birth of a special child and reflections on the death of a much-loved aunt …

They will be read and enjoyed by a large following of her regular readers and others.

CONTENTS

FOREWORD

I WOULD not have known if I had not been told — by one of my early teachers, Miss Margaret Adie — that, by the age of eight or nine, I was already telling the class that I wanted to be a journalist. She was a young teacher at Rathen School, near Fraserburgh, at the time and I, briefly, one of her pupils.

My schooldays there were few because transport links from Crimond School to home at Lonmay were better. We had moved from Stuartfield, where I was born, to Lonmay, nearer the coast, just before the outbreak of World War II.

The war was over by the time the family settled at Strichen in 1946 and by then I was already attending Fraserburgh Academy. In her retirement, Miss Adie lived in Aberdeen and did not forget her erstwhile pupil.

In a letter to me in 1988, she wrote: "I remember once asking Ian Taggart, Alex Lee, Doris Campbell, Richard Lee and all their classmates, what they would like to be when they grew up.

"There were various replies, ranging from the engine-driver beloved of all boys at school. But one that struck me as unusual in its finality from one so young came from Pearl Murray, who knew thus early that she wanted to be a journalist."

Of course, I have no recollection of it. An early interest, on my part, in current affairs was noted, though. Older relatives have said that, even as a little girl, I was more likely to be caught up in Picture Post than in Mickey Mouse or Girls' Own, or any other comic.

If they predicted from that any kind of academic aptitude, they were to be disappointed. Academic, I am not — a fact which became fairly clear at Fraserburgh Academy. I was completely incapable of mastering mathematics. Once, in an algebra exam, I was awarded a total of half a mark out of 50 for writing my name clearly at the top of the paper.

On another occasion, daydreaming in an arithmetic class, the teacher brought me down to earth with a jolt:

"How many yards in a pole?" he demanded, banging his pointer on the desk.

"Depends on the length of the pole," I blurted out without thinking.

For once, I did know the answer and could have given it if I had had time to think, but the poor teacher could hardly be blamed for assuming otherwise.

In fact, I enjoyed my schooldays at Fraserburgh very much. I liked languages and revelled in English and, with the minimum of effort, I somehow managed to end up with an excellent education.

For that, I have always been grateful to teachers such as Mr Edwin Johnston (Geography), Miss Gladys Minty (Modern Languages), Mr James Lessells (Classics), Mr Stewart Robertson (English) and Miss May C. Jenkins (History) — she, later to be a colleague at Aberdeen Journals.

I must mention an inspired teacher of English, Mr Ben B. Smith, whom I first encountered when I was struggling vainly with maths and losing interest rapidly in most school work. Eventually, he became director of education for Kincardine but, at Fraserburgh, he took a keen interest in my English and especially my essay-writing, always encouraging and urging me to do better. But for him, I might well have given up and might never have had the career I did.

By the end of the fifth year, I had made up my mind to leave school. I had intimated my intention to the rector, Mr W.D. Kennedy, who was well aware of what I wanted to do. He summoned me to his office. I can see him still, a grey-haired, slightly built, distinguished figure with piercing brown eyes.

He waited until I was seated comfortably. "So you want to leave school?" he began. Then he launched into every reason why I should not.

He advised me strongly to take a sixth year and study a science subject for university entrance. Forget about journalism. "You need a lot of luck for that," he warned.

"You should go to university and take a degree in English. You'll have to work harder than you've done here, but I'm sure you could do it. It would give you much more security ..."

His voice trailed off. He could see from my expression. "So be it," he concluded. I had made up my mind. Irrevocably.

What he did not know then was that I had already taken advice from William Veitch, at that time editor-in-chief of Aberdeen Journals, who agreed that there was no better training for journalism than hands-on experience on weekly newspapers. That was probably true then. It is not the advice I would give today.

What I did not know was that jobs for trainee reporters were not exactly thick on the ground in the early 1950s. In fact, it was to be a year or more before I was offered an opening at Turriff, which began a career on weekly newspapers on which I learned the job and which took me from Turriff to Banff and Inverurie and finally to the old Bon-Accord in Aberdeen.

As it turned out, I was glad of that respite between school and journalism. To fill my days, I took a temporary office job with the Fraserburgh branch of a national fish-curing firm. That is how I came to follow the silver darlings, with a lot of other North-east folk, down the coast to Lowestoft.

My sojourn in England lasted, I suppose, for three or four months, and I have some very good reasons to be thankful for it. The first is that I lived with, worked with and came to respect those kindly fisher folk from the coastal towns and villages of the North-east who are the backbone of Buchan as much as their agricultural contemporaries.

My admiration grew by the day as I watched them put out in tiny boats in seas which were truly awesome. Yet, never did I hear a serious moan or grumble — and that when lives, not crops, were at stake. I watched the fisherwomen in the gutting sheds, their hands frozen to the bone, endure a daily darg with cheerfulness in awful conditions which were smelly, as well as wet, and very cold. I heard them singing to help pass the slow hours.

The best-known story of Buchan tells how our predecessors broke their backs in transforming a tract of barren land into the most fertile piece of farming country in Scotland. The other story, not yet told, is of the hard-working, God-fearing, stoic fishing communities whose people are a race apart.

Another reason why I am pleased to have had that stay in

Suffolk is that it introduced me to the English. I am not sure what I expected; they are not the most popular people on earth with the Scots. I got on well with them; very well, indeed.

That is why I am uneasy about the current White Settler business. It is racist — and that is always dangerous. I do understand the local resentment when well-heeled incomers beat the local people to their crofts and houses. On the other hand, the Scots have, throughout history, been successful opportunists and, had the boot been on the other foot, I am quite sure we would not have hesitated to do likewise.

Another grudge is that, according to the received wisdom, our English neighbours come into Scottish communities and tend to take over. Is it not that it takes a fresh eye to see what needs to be done? In any case, we ought, I think, to be receptive to new ideas, fresh thinking and different viewpoints, without in any way forfeiting our own culture. How else can we develop?

At the end of the day, nobody can deny that, in many cases, the arrival of our English friends has breathed new life into some communities which, otherwise, had not much prospect ...

I know, in retrospect, that I still had stars in my eyes when I began my career on local papers in the early 1950s. Nothing could have prepared me for the long hours and the low pay which was the reporter's lot on weekly papers. I was 22 years old and working for the Bon-Accord before I could stand on my own feet financially, without being subsidised by my father.

If I remember rightly, my first week's pay was £2 and a few shillings, a handsome total which did not even cover the cost of lodgings. What my generation of trainee reporters was doing was virtually paying for what training there was on weekly newspapers by their sheer hard graft — and with precious little money to show for it.

The work was as varied as it was hard and the chance to cover everything was the true value of the training. There were meetings to be reported (usually in the evenings), courts, sales of work, Burns Suppers, agricultural shows, ploughing matches ... and the dreaded obituaries to be compiled about prominent local people who had passed on.

A common North-east ritual in those days was viewing the

corpse and this, on several occasions, I was invited to do on a visit to the deceased's home to garner information for the tribute. Most of the time, my refusal was accepted without demur. Except once, when a distraught widow took it badly: "If he's nae good enough ti look at, he's nae good enough ti write aboot," she snapped.

She ushered me into the parlour where lay her husband in his last sleep. "Affa like himsel, isn't he?" she remarked. I would not have known, for my eyes were tight shut and, in any case, I never knew him.

There was a lot of fun, too, often shared with colleagues Jimmy Gorrie and Bob Carter from the nearby Banffshire Journal. They were not with me on two occasions which — amusing in retrospect — tempted me to think that my old headmaster was right: I should have opted for the gentle groves of Academe.

One editor, who shall be nameless, liked to roll his own cigarettes and seemed to spend more time trying to light them than in actually smoking them. He liked, also, to imbibe freely from a bottle secreted in a drawer.

We shared an editorial office and one day, returning from an afternoon assignment, I found him slumped, head in arms, over his desk. Leaving him to it, I settled to write when, suddenly, his wastepaper basket caught fire, setting alight a bundle of newspapers beside it. The conflagration was as quick as it was frightening, extinguished eventually by frantic workers bearing buckets of water.

A smouldering fag end, a hot match tossed away carelessly, whatever it was, the culprit was bundled home to sleep it off but, believe it or not, not even that episode taught him a lesson. Merely a matter of months afterwards, he was in a similar state on one publication night and quite unable to put the paper to bed.

It came off the presses eventually, many hours late, and I was press-ganged into driving the proprietor's car, with bundles of papers in the boot, delivering them off through the night at newspaper shops over a large, rural area. Worse still, I was assigned on the way, to drop off a drunken effigy into the arms of an incensed wife, nursing her wrath to keep it warm.

"Fit kinna state's at ti get him intil?" she bellowed, as if I were personally responsible. I was not enchanted.

By the time I joined Aberdeen Journals in 1955, I was a confident reporter and an adequate sub-editor — which was a good start. My aim was to be a writer. I wanted to write feature articles under my own name and, perhaps one day, a column.

Three years later, the chance came when I was made woman's editor of the Evening Express, which involved writing signed feature articles, basically on subjects aimed at women. In addition, I was given my own column, mainly showbiz in content, featuring visiting stars of stage, screen and from the world of pop music.

That was my introduction to many of the famous and some of the rich, for in those days most of the major stars of the British stage came to HM Theatre in Aberdeen. Hardly a household name was there that I did not interview in the six years I wrote the People I Meet column for the city's evening newspaper.

I remember the impressive Paul Robeson as much for his intellect as for his marvellous voice; the intense Margaret Lockwood and her daughter Julia; the charming Anna Neagle; the merry Jean Kent; the delightful Dulcie Gray and her handsome husband, Michael Denison; the temperamental Alma Cogan; the bubbly Tommy Steele, the caring Frankie Vaughan ... there is simply no space to mention more than a handful.

Showbiz people are generally a warm-hearted lot. The huge efforts they put in for charity, especially for children, testify to that. I have to say, though, that as I interviewed them on a one-to-one basis every week, disillusion set in. It was almost impossible to discover what the real person was like underneath the image — such was the affectation, the ego, the image-consciousness. Too often, I am afraid, they tended to come across as cardboard characters who had spent too much time reading and believing their own publicity.

The stars of showbiz were not the only prominent people to come within our orbit as journalists. Celebrated musicians, noted writers and national politicians came and went, towering figures such as the late Lord Grimond and the Iron Lady herself. Margaret Thatcher was leader of the Opposition when I interviewed her in Aberdeen at the end of what was for her a gruelling North-east tour.

I could have been put off, marginally, by the presence of her image-maker, Gordon (now Sir Gordon) Reece, who sat in and recorded every word of the interview. "Have you got enough for your story?" Britain's future prime minister inquired solicitously at the end. I found her a much warmer, softer person than came across, even then, on television.

The lives of the glitzy rich, the ephemeral stars, did not impress me at all. Their lives were as tinsel compared to the lives of ordinary people, living ordinary lives, often against the odds and in extraordinary circumstances. Theirs was — and remains — the real story.

By 1964, when I switched to the Press and Journal, I already had a career which had given me a first-class air ticket to many parts of the world, a ringside seat at every major event in the North and North-east and a free pass to almost any national occasion I cared to attend. There were times when I could not believe that I was actually being paid for what, in other circumstances, I would have done gladly for nothing.

Not being an investigative reporter worth a farthing, I began to relish making what I thought was a positive contribution by trying to expose injustice and hardship wherever I found it. These, I realised quickly, were often the undeserved lot of disabled people and I did not hear many influential voices raised on their behalf.

Once, watching the experts training dogs for the blind at Forfar and, noting the long list of blind people in Scotland waiting for a dog, I was moved to consider what could be done through the newspaper to help. First, I tested the water with a personal Christmas appeal for money to train one dog — £250, the amount it cost, was a lot of money in those days.

Enough flooded in to train nine dogs, and the significant thing was the number of children who had become involved. This, in turn, led to a full-scale campaign at the end of the 1960s which mobilised, through the newspaper, the efforts of youngsters throughout the northern half of Scotland to raise money to train those gentle animals.

I travelled many thousands of miles promoting the appeal, to many parts of the Highlands, to the North and to the magical isles of Orkney and Shetland, whose hospitality and kindness I will never forget.

The response to the appeal was magnificent. A total of £21,741 was raised, enough to give a dog to every blind person in Scotland who was waiting for one. What, I wonder, would that amount be worth in today's money?

"Why did you never leave the North-east?" I am often asked. I could have left, it is true. Over the years, I had offers of editorial posts which would have taken me to Edinburgh or Glasgow; to Manchester or London. I stayed because the clichéd name in lights and a small fortune (even if they were possibilities) were not among my priorities. Certainly, they are not usually the rewards of a career on provincial newspapers.

I do not mind in the least being regarded as "provincial". Why should I? Nobody ever told me that the landscapes of the mind are constrained by geographical boundaries.

The quality of life exists still in the North-east which I was, years ago, reluctant to forfeit for a career on national newspapers. I have no regrets. Now, in retirement, as I walk my dogs over the Deeside moors, I reflect on the good fortune which has allowed me to live and work amid such splendour.

That luck, which my old headmaster predicted I would need, has been mine — in abundance.

Pearl Murray
September, 1994

BACK TO BUCHAN

TOMORROW, I will take the old, familiar road to Buchan by way of Balmedie and Ellon and, one way or another, on to Mintlaw, not a million miles from where I was born in the pretty village of Stuartfield. Green and lush at this time of year is the level landscape, alight in patches with the yellow of whin and bracken and the bright, new-fangled crops of rape.

A douce and smiling countryside it is in the summer, with not a hint of the wicked winds and killing cold which so ravage it in winter.

In no time at all, there will be the bridge at Ellon and the usual choice of roads to take. Will it be the back one which meanders gently by Auchnagatt to Stuartfield and Old Deer? Or the main Aberdeen-Fraserburgh highway, by the Toll of Birness and Ardallie to Mintlaw?

My favourite, by far, is the slower, country road, although I know every inch of them both and nostalgia for me is a journey on either. But the decision depends on time — the time of the year and the time available more immediately.

If, at summer's end, the harvest is upon us and the parks stretch like a cloth of gold over the world's edge, I can think of few delights to compare with wandering at will by the back road through those pastoral places, enjoying the lift of the sky and the endless horizons, savouring the sense of freedom and space.

There, by the roadside at Auchnagatt, Mains of Annochie, the farm where, on wartime holidays, the plaintive choruses of cornkisters first reached my ears and the realisation dawned that other races lived beyond the seas, as Italian prisoners were dragooned to help the war effort on the land.

Then on to my birthplace of "Crichie", as it is called in these parts. Somehow, the years retreat and I am back once more in the little classroom of the local school, listening to the voice of Miss Minty, my first headmistress. Nothing more clearly recalls my early days than the Doric spoken by genuine Buchan voices. And, with a pang, in the selective way of remembered childhood, the folk seem the best; the old scenes somehow brightest.

I am always pleased to take the road back to Buchan for the simple reason that it takes me home. I don't expect, however, that there will be lot of time for nostalgia tomorrow, for I am going there for a purpose — to open the Aden Farm and Field Day at the Aden Country Park, Old Deer.

As readers of this column might know, the country park and agricultural-heritage centre is now probably the top leisure attraction in Grampian and I have congratulated Banff and Buchan District Council on its huge success publicly before.

It draws more than 100,000 visitors every year and they can enjoy country pursuits in the park such as fishing and pony-trekking and, browsing through the heritage centre, they can take in two permanent exhibitions, both displayed extremely professionally.

One, based on the accounts of workers on the old Aden Estate, shows what life was like on a rural estate at the turn of the century. The other highlights 200 years of radical change in farming methods, and this celebrates the making of Buchan.

The romance of that particular story, of course, is how a rugged and industrious people transformed a poor and stony place into one of the biggest, richest tracts of farming land in Scotland.

The park and heritage centre, however, are part of a wider concept. The hope is to link the estate exhibition by signposts to the estate village of Old Deer nearby, where it is relatively well preserved under a conservation order. Another idea is to breathe life into the farming exhibition by building a working croft in the park.

That was the brainchild of Mr Andrew Hill, the centre's enthusiastic young curator, who soon won over to his way of thinking Mr Gil Carling, the district council's director of leisure and recreation, and Mr Bill Cruickshank, the public-spirited farmer who is chairman of the Aden Park Committee.

The problem, clearly, is the cost and, as far as I know, the district council has not yet made a decision about the working croft which, together with incorporating Old Deer, would make Aden a country-life centre of national importance. More immediately, it will tomorrow be the venue for the district council's Aden Farm and Field Day, which has become a very popular annual event and attracts crowds from a' the airts. There will be pipe bands and majorettes, heavy horses and sheepdogs and gleaming farm equipment from past and present.

For all the reasons I have mentioned, I am delighted to be going, to be among my ain folk. But there is another reason which is probably the most important of all, and that is that the proceeds are going to handicapped people in Banff and Buchan.

You see, I happen to agree with Mrs Thatcher, who thinks that charity begins at home. In fact, in some respects I am quite a fan of the Iron Lady and, I assure you, she is a much warmer, softer person in the flesh than her media image suggests.

However, I cannot condone the materialistic "loadsamoney" society, if only because so many are left out in the cold. Ask the unemployed, the single parent, the many thousands who, non-unionised, are exploited ruthlessly by employers who call themselves respectable.

The old and infirm and the handicapped ... how they are treated says a lot about our society. And what does it say about us?

June 11, 1988

● *The working croft — since this was written — has become a reality. It was built in 1991, moved stone by stone from Hareshowe of Ironside, New Deer, of which old croft it is an exact replica. Not surprisingly, it has become one of the top attractions at Aden Park, drawing more than 12,000 visitors last year.*

Many of them saw the summer demonstrations of such farming activities as harrowing and shimming the neeps and, in November, the ploughing, all done by horses worked by Britain's top horseman, Jim Elliott, South Knaven, Auchnagatt. What a nostalgic sight it is.

Fit is't like?

ME? Write a cookery column? I could not conceal my discomfiture. Cooking was something I did only when I had to, in emergencies. It was not something I had to do very often. As a working woman, I ate out most of the time.

Me? Write a cookery column? It was preposterous.

"Well, you don't actually have to write it …"

The Editor was persuasive.

"You just have to choose some recipes once a week. Stacks of them come in regularly from people like flour manufacturers, margarine makers and the Egg Marketing Board. You don't even have to try them out; most of them are tested already. All I'm asking you to do is make a weekly selection.

"Oh, and try to introduce something different. A change from mince and tatties, you know."

The year was 1964 and the assignment seemed an inauspicious beginning to my new job, working in the cosy old office in Broad Street, Aberdeen, where now stands the new Town House.

By that time, the more adventurous and those who could afford it were already deserting Costa Collieston to spend their precious summer fortnight in warmer climes, returning with the obligatory tan and souvenir sombreros or garish flamenco dolls.

For most, the big night out was tea at Strathdee's or Mitchell and Muil's. Egg, bacon and chips or the like, washed down with nothing stronger than the cup that cheers. This was followed often by a visit to the cinema.

Or sometimes, the flicks came first, and afterwards, maybe, a carry-out supper of pie, pudding or fish, for those were the days when this was the extent of the menu in the ubiquitous fish-and-chip shops.

High tea, nowadays all but extinct, was still the evening meal throughout the North-east, eaten usually around 5-5.30pm — a single cooked course of macaroni-cheese, or maybe scrambled or boiled eggs, followed by masses of carbohydrates in home-baked scones, pancakes and other goodies. Calorie-counting was nothing like as important then as now.

Against this background, my first cooking columns appeared. Nothing adventurous at first, merely variations on well-known themes. But the time soon came to be a little bolder. I introduced garlic — at least, I reasoned, those who had been abroad would know it.

Predictably, the phone rang a few times that morning, with calls mainly from readers asking where they could buy it and how much of it they would use.

Then a greengrocer telephoned from a Buchan village. Let's say it was Mintlaw.

"Is 'at you that writes 'at rubbish aboot cookin' in the paper?" he inquired tactfully.

"Weel, I've hid a puckle wifies in 'is mornin askin aboot 'at stuff … garlic. Could ye tell's mair aboot it? I'll need ti get some in, and it's nae grown hereaboots.

"Is't like a neep or an ingin?"

April 10, 1989

LOVE AFFAIR

ONE of my early memories is of sitting, all wrapped up, in the dickey seat of an old Ford car— well, perhaps it was not really old and maybe it was not a Ford. I remember the rushing wind as we chugged through the dark, the march of the trees, the canopy of stars, the sharp smell of leather mingling with petrol fumes, the sense of adventure.

On nocturnal journeys, we hoped secretly that the noisy, spluttering engine would stop and that wc would be stranded in the night, miles from a telephone and hours from home. It was not a prospect relished by the driver who, on such occasions, had to try to coax the hulk to life by frantic cranking of the starting handle.

The dickey seat became synonymous with seaside Sundays or summer holidays, when we would set off, small suitcases packed around our legs. But more than that, it was in the dickey seat that my love affair with cars began. Other girls longed to own a horse or priceless jewellery or aspired to travel the world. My teenage passion was for a car. Not just any car — it had to be a sports car, with the hood down and the rushing wind to remind me of the dickey seat of my childhood.

World War II was barely six years gone and cars of any kind — let alone sports cars — were not exactly thick on the ground. In fact, in our village at that time, there was only one female driver, I think, until I passed my test. That day, I set off in a borrowed car to confront the examiner, and quite a heart-stopping day it turned out to be. First, the family car I had been using for practice let me down. It was, I remember, a stubborn, unwieldy monster, which failed to respond to towing and pushing and cranking.

To top it all, there was then some query about documentation, which the examiner — a silent but friendly chap — quickly sorted out. At last, the test went ahead and it was a measure of my youthful arrogance that nervous I was not. Come to think of it, it was not arrogance. My confidence was rooted in lots of experience.

Since I had been knee-high to a bumper, I had been driving at every opportunity — small cars, large cars, old cars and new cars, even the occasional tractor — wherever my unlicensed practice was not breaking the law.

Besides, my brother, Kenny, (who could handle a car better than anyone I know) had been coaching me patiently and had taught me all there was to know about driving, as well as something about the intricate workings of the petrol engine.

In fact, long before I presented myself for the test, I could (among other things) set sparking plugs, clean a carburettor and change a wheel. Today, I can do none of these things — to my shame, I have even to consult the handbook to know how to open the bonnet.

I learned also to recognise the warning noises of breakdown — the rumble of a back end, for instance. Even now, I find myself listening intently to the changing notes of an aircraft engine, praying that they are no threat.

Some prestige was attached then, as now, to passing the test first time. In my case, however, rather more than that hinged on my success. There was that car. I fancied an MGTC model of blessed memory, but the machine I had my eye on was something else.

It belonged to a doctor who lived not far away and I saw it frequently. It was shining red with enormous silver exhausts along the side and a tail like the back end of a submarine. The bonnet was tied down with straps and the red interior leather shone like the paintwork, a perfect foil for the classy cream steering wheel. It was a Riley Brooklands Special and, I am told, not many were made.

"You always remember your first car," the owner told me as he handed over the keys, "and you will never forget this one."

For a couple of years or so, we toured the highways and byways, me and my spaniel friend in the little red car. Then, one day, as we were moving off, the dog — spotting a mate across the road — tried to leap out.

For days, I agonised over which should go although, of course, there was no choice. The day I parted with my little red car was the day I grew up. With it went part of my heart and the happy, carefree days of my youth.

That day, too, my love affair with cars came to an end. Even now, I think of it with nostalgia, for — apart from the fun we had together — it taught me self-discipline, road manners and an early awareness of the dangers of speed.

It was believed that my car belonged originally to Nazi leader, Hermann Goering, and that it was laid up during World War II at the engineering works of Krupps in Essen. I have not found out whether this is true or not.

I do not pay much attention to modern models any more which, I suppose, says more about me than it does about the manufacturers' designers, who spend so many thousands on shape and colour and style and so on.

I am simply not tempted — except, at the occasional rally, when I happen to catch sight of a jaunty old jalopy with a dickey seat. My heart leaps and I feel again the excitement and mystery; the rush of wind on my face. I see again the march of the trees and the bright canopy of stars. Which is where it began all those years ago.

And, by the way, parting with my little red car was not my smartest move; I have it on the best authority that, had I kept it, it would have been the best investment I ever made.

July 20, 1991

CULLODEN

BLOOD, they say, is thicker than water and so are the bonds of family, of name and of common descent which held together the old Scottish clans. It was something of the kind, something perhaps carried down in the genes, which sent me on a journey the other day which was nothing short of a pilgrimage.

Lowering clouds and squalls of hail driven by a biting wind and turning occasionally to snow made the day as cruel as the cruellest in April and, beyond Nairn, the outline of the mountains emerged, dusted icing-white.

On a day like this, 242 years ago, the gallant tartan army of Prince Charles Edward Stuart lined up on a bare Scottish moor for the last great battle fought on British soil. The lieutenant-general of the prince's men, of the starved and weary clansmen, was Lord George Murray. With a name like mine, who could be inured to Culloden?

This was not my first visit to the battlefield. I had been when the moor was covered in trees and a road ran through the graves of the clansmen as if an attempt had been made to forget; to pretend that nothing so vile had ever happened here.

There was an aura in the enfolding trees, whose branches lent a shadowy melancholy, and there is an aura still. The grassy mounds of the clan graves are green and gentle, marked by rough stones with weathered letters. It is striking in its simplicity; moving in its understatement.

The offending road no longer runs through the graves and the trees have been felled to lay bare a moor bounded in the distance by the green waters of the Moray Firth on the one hand and by a snow-tipped range of hills on the other. The National Trust for Scotland has made the battlefield very much more like it was on that day so long ago, and it is easier now to visualise the battle and the background to it.

That is what pilgrims to Culloden try to imagine, and about 218,000 of them came last year, most English, then Scots, followed by Americans and visitors from the Commonwealth, particularly Canada, Australia and New Zealand.

The battle itself drew sightseers those long years ago. People came from Inverness and around, including Elizabeth, daughter of Duncan Campbell of Clunas, who hoped to marry the mighty MacGillivray of Dunmaglass.

He charged with such ferocity that, leaping over his slain as he went, he broke through Cumberland's first line before falling himself. His body was found near the Well of the Dead.

In the heather, half a dozen truant schoolboys, mostly the sons of clan chiefs, had come to watch their kinsmen in battle. They included nine-year-old Archibald Fraser, whose brother, the Master of Lovat, was somewhere among the clansmen; Arthur, son of the Laird of Inshes, and young James Mackintosh of Farr, who lived to be 90, but who never forgot the look on his father's face as he watched him march by at the head of his regiment. He never saw his father again.

Besides, some beggars from the surrounding countryside arrived to loot. The motley lot loitered around the battlefield perimeter, listening to the assembled clansmen singing as they awaited Cumberland's fire. Dispirited and outnumbered, they sang the Twentieth Psalm:

Jehovah hear thee in the day
When trouble He doth send ...

Almost 250 years on, countless numbers regard Culloden Field as part of their heritage. Above all, when they come, overseas visitors want to know about the involvement of their own clan. If it turns out to be a non-Jacobite one, their disappointment is intense.

Such is the lustre with which a lost causes seizes the imagination. Although it ended forever the claim of the Catholic Stuarts to the throne, the battle had all the elements of romance — a dashing hero in the Bonnie Prince (whatever the verdict of history) and an ignoble villain in Butcher Cumberland, whose savagery in the aftermath remains such a shameful blot on British military conduct that, according to historian John Prebble, no British regiment has Culloden among its battle honours.

The most common misconception to this day is that the battle

*My Riley Brooklands Special, of which only a few were made.
See P20.*

*Meeting Princess Alexandra at a Guide Dog reception in Aberdeen
in 1969. See P98*

My friend, Christopher (2), a small boy with a very big presence.
See P31.

Liz Marshall, of Musselburgh, with Shera, my beautiful wonder-dog.
See P34.

was a Scottish-English encounter. It was nothing of the sort. Not all the clans, by any means, threw their weight behind the prince, and there were Highlanders in Cumberland's army.

The clansmen's allegiance was determined by diverse factors such as politics or religion, or simply that they had been ordered by their chief — under the patriarchal system of the clan — to fight.

It was, of course, a battle in a civil war in which father fought against son and brother against brother. Sometimes, to ensure survival, a chief would send one son to fight with the prince and other to march with Cumberland's men.

The redoubtable Lady Mackintosh of Moy Hall, known to history as Colonel Anne, waited until her husband had gone to command a company for King George. No sooner had he departed than his spirited, 20-year-old wife raised his clansmen for the prince, calling them from the hills and glens, giving each a white cockade and finally, in blue bonnet and tartan riding clothes, riding at their head to the prince.

Afterwards, on that field of death where at least 1,000 of the prince's men lay slain or murdered, James and John Chisholm, who fought for Cumberland, found their younger brother surrounded by the fallen of nearly all their clan. They washed the boy's face, straightened his limbs and stood guard over his body to protect it from mutilation.

At Culloden today, on the precise anniversary of the battle, the Gaelic Society of Inverness are holding a commemorative service, as they do every year on the Saturday nearest the date.

A wreath will be laid; prayers said; a piper's lament will echo across the moor, and the society chief will pay tribute to the fallen, in Gaelic and English. The chief, Mr John MacKay, of North Kessock, is symbolic of the new, united Highland community. The MacKays were on the Government side, while the Macleans, his mother's clan, fought for the prince.

For the record, Lord George Murray survived the slaughter. If his advice had been taken, the course of history might have been changed. If he had not escaped with some of his clan, I might not be here to tell the tale.

April 16, 1988

TOP GUN?

FOR a long time, there was this recurring nightmare of a long, straight stretch of road and the menacing shape of an enemy bomber, roaring over at treetop height, its guns blazing. Not all nightmares have their origins in reality, but this one had — and it persisted, as I remember, for quite a long time.

It happened during World War II. At that time, my home was at Lonmay, in the quiet countryside between Fraserburgh and Peterhead, near the coast on that knuckle of Aberdeenshire which juts into the North Sea and which was to become known as Hellfire Corner.

Our little school, at Crimond, about midway between the two towns, was near an RAF aerodrome — or was it Fleet Air Arm? I'm not sure, because I was not then 10 years old; while some incidents stand out with amazing clarity, others are hazy and less distinct.

I cannot think why we were allowed, in those dangerous days, to cycle to and from school — perhaps the bus service was erratic — but almost all of us did, and thought nothing of it. Not that it took very long to cycle the couple of miles or so, unless we dallied, which we did often on the way home.

That is what we were doing one day after school. The boys, including my brother, Kenny, were trying to race each other on their bikes up and down a shallow burn, unable to balance for more than a minute, falling off into the water with loud shrieks and splashes, while the girls watched from the bridge.

The innocent fun was interrupted by the noise of an aircraft flying low. A Spitfire had appeared from nowhere, its engine spluttering, white smoke gushing from behind as it gradually lost height and vanished over some trees. We expected the bang which soon came and were already on our bikes, pedalling furiously towards it, when a large pall of smoke rose on the horizon.

Either the farmer or the police were on the scene first — I

cannot remember which — but we, curious children, were not long behind. Excited by the drama, we had hurried to the scene only to be kept back from the smouldering wreck. Young as we were, our mood changed quickly as we watched the pilot's body lifted from the cockpit and laid gently on the field.

It was the first time in my young life that I had encountered death and, in that instant, I understood the meaning of war.

Daily, at school, we were reminded what to do in the event of an invasion. After all, we were nearer to German-occupied Norway than almost anywhere else in Britain. If it happened during the day, we were told to take to the fields and make for home as fast as we could.

The classroom walls were hung with large posters depicting the uniforms of the three enemy Services and we were taught to recognise them. But rarely was the enemy referred to as anything other than "the Hun" or "the Bosch". To our young minds, a "good" German was as unlikely a phenomenon as a white blackbird.

At home, calm prevailed, at least on the surface. In retrospect, I guess it was sometimes feigned. As children, we sensed the tension when, for instance, the radio news was bad or when, sitting by the fire in the blacked-out evening, we identified the distinctive drone of an enemy plane.

Pleasures were simple then, and largely home-produced. One highlight was a rollicking concert staged by the WRI in the local hall. We were driven there by hired car, its masked headlights picking out the dim way. Then, on the way back, there was childish excitement as the tracery of bullets from a dogfight over a coastal convoy lit up the night sky like an impressive display of fireworks.

I am indebted to Sue Lawley, TV's First Lady, for her masterly presentation last week of the news as it broke exactly 50 years ago. In the orgy of nostalgia which marked the outbreak of World War II, she brought back for me the tenor of that time more acutely than any of the popular songs, or the old, familiar voices, evocative though they were.

Of the memories she stirred, none in my case was the stuff of nightmares ... except one. There was this straight stretch of road bordered by trees. We were cycling home after school, a little crocodile of children on bicycles. We had just entered the straight when, suddenly, an enemy bomber appeared from nowhere at the far end.

It roared towards us at treetop level. Instinctively, we leaped from our bikes into the roadside ditch, covering our heads with our hands, as we had been taught. The noise was deafening as the plane passed over, its guns spitting, spraying the road and the trees with bullets.

Trembling, we lay there until we were sure it wasn't going to make another run. But it did not and we pedalled home furiously with a tale to tell. It was, I think, the first time in my life that I knew real fear, and I was to relive the episode in bad dreams for a long time.

The long, straight stretch and the trees are there to this day and I was often to wonder what kind of enemy it was who would gun down innocent children. The war was over a decade and more before I made my first trip to Germany, on a Press visit to the Gordon Highlanders, who were stationed at Celle as part of the British Army of the Rhine.

So effective was wartime brainwashing that, even then, I was still struggling with my own prejudice. Sunday was a day off and an officer suggested that I might like to see Belsen. The notorious concentration camp had been turned into a memorial to those who had perished there.

I was given a British Army car and two Jocks as escort and we set off that sunny Sunday on a strange pilgrimage.

Lots of cars were parked by the entrance, along with some touring coaches. But I was not prepared for what was going on inside. There was no reverence. Instead, German families picnicked on grassy mounds, kicked coloured balls, drank wine and joked.

The mounds were the mass graves.

It took a long time to forgive. But I have not forgotten.

September 9, 1989

CHRISTOPHER

I AM TOTALLY captivated by a young man called Christopher. He is coming at Christmas and he is very special. If you read on, I will tell you why. But first, let me say that, as the recession continues on its cruel course, I am well aware that there will be many thousands of people across the country who are not looking forward to Christmas as I am. They are those who, in these hard times, have lost their jobs through no fault of their own or who have seen their businesses, their lives' work, go to the wall.

There are others, too, dreading the possible loss of their livelihoods, whose anxiety makes it impossible to participate wholeheartedly in the festive celebrations. No doubt they will make the best of it and put on a brave face, if only for the children. The reality, though, is that Christmas will be less than festive in more homes this year than anyone really knows.

Annus horribilis is how Her Majesty described the dying year recently — and it has been just that for many of her subjects, too, as the Queen was quick to acknowledge.

The true meaning of Christmas is — I hear you protest — not about material things and what you can buy, however. It is about the Christ Child and his birthday. It is, above all, a religious occasion with children at its heart. Of course, it is.

But how do you explain that to children of this day and age, who identify Christmas with commercialism and spending and more and bigger expensive gifts? How do you tell a child that he will not be getting what his playmates will be getting, because Daddy has no job, so there is no money to spare?

That cannot be easy. Nor is it easy to explain that everything is relative and that, in global terms, it is only a small hardship. Compared to some of the ills of the world, it is nothing. A child's experience, however, does not stretch to encompass the horror of starving masses dying in Ethiopia or Bosnia or anywhere else.

31

This anecdote, true or apocryphal, puts it neatly: "Eat up your food," a mother remonstrates with her child who is reluctant to clean his plate. "Think of the starving children of Ethiopia," she exhorts.

"Name one!" comes the telling reply.

This year, our Christmas promises to be special, not because of material things or an excess of anything, but because of something priceless that no money can buy; something much nearer the true meaning of this Holy time.

Christopher is coming to visit at Christmas. By then, he will be just five months and a few days old; a very small boy with a very big presence. He is special, not simply for himself, but because he is something of a miracle. His mother, in her late 40s, knew from the start that the risk to them both was high because of her age. In the event, Christopher was born a lovely, healthy baby, but serious complications followed the birth and his mother almost died.

In intensive care, she clung desperately to life, knowing that her tiny son was alive and well. For us, who are her friends, the trembling hours were slow and fearful and all we could do was pray. Baby Christopher, in the hospital nursery, slept on, blissfully unaware of the drama. But the hearts of a succession of kindly nurses went out to the solitary bundle, wrapping him securely in their loving care, tending to his every need. Some volunteered to wash his clothes, which was not within the bounds of duty; others, in the long watches of night in the ward, knitted for him out of the goodness of their hearts.

All this was just part of the great outpouring of kindness and warmth which surrounded the brave mother as she set out on the long, hard road to recovery. The hospital had to ask the florists to stagger the deliveries of flowers, which were arriving in such thick abundance that the hospital could not cope.

Now do you see why we are redecorating the house with renewed enthusiasm this year? It is almost 30 years since children came at Christmas, my nieces and nephews, adults themselves now.

There was always a a Christmas party, although not necessarily on the day itself, with all the traditional trappings and a tree with presents piled below. One memorable day, Santa himself appeared. We heard his bell and saw him plodding up the brae in front of the house. Kindly he was, and full of good cheer as he dispensed the parcels, one by one from the tree, sometimes sitting with a child on either knee, their eyes wide with wonder.

Then the eldest, who in any case had his suspicions about Santa, whispered: "Auntie, is that David's voice?" I pinched him hard and winked and he said no more, not wishing to mar the moment for the younger ones. Sadly, David Benzie, our friendly neighbour, is no longer with us, but he is remembered fondly by my nieces and nephews as is his widow, Olga, who still lives next door.

Christopher, sunny and sociable, will evoke many memories such as these. But he is of yet another generation, a citizen of the next century, who might one day buy a ticket to the moon.

For the moment, he is too young to know much about this, his first Christmas, or about the gaily wrapped parcels with his presents. He will have toys, of course, but the presents we really want for him are those beyond price — health and happiness and fulfilment for as long as he lives.

December 19, 1992

● *Christopher's mother has made a full recovery and she is justifiably proud of her little boy, whose engaging personality has won him many friends, including me.*

DEAR SHERA

NOBODY knew her name or how old she was or where exactly she had come from. To this day, nobody knows, but they called her Shera, after some cartoon character. I know not why; there had been certainly nothing funny about her life.

You might remember a lovely German Shepherd dog whose pictures appeared in the Press and Journal a few years ago. As I recall, there was nothing particularly dramatic in the paper that day, except the usual wars and rumours of war.

Then, on an inside page, I saw her. There she was with puppies around her, her lovely face gazing out of the page. She looked content and secure, but she had a haunted look which I could not get out of my mind. I knew then that this was the beginning for Shera and me.

The report described how this extraordinary dog and her nine puppies had been found under a gorse bush on a Dundee golf course, surrounded by lots of empty milk cartons. Emaciated and on the point of starvation, she had been taken with her brood to the German Shepherd Dog Rescue kennels at Darnabo Croft, Fyvie, into the care of Mrs Sue Tulloch.

Shera had been abandoned and ill-treated. She had been cast out, left to roam, to exist on whatever scraps she could find. Inevitably, she often had nothing to eat.

At last, wearily, she had found some sanctuary, although little shelter, under a bush to rear her young. At the time they were discovered, rescuers thought the pups were only a week old.

Thus far, there is nothing particularly remarkable or unusual in Shera's story. Sadly, what happened to her happens to many hundreds of dogs every day in this animal-loving nation of ours. That is why almost every breed now has its own set-up to rescue, to care for, and ultimately to find homes for hapless creatures abandoned so wantonly and wilfully.

What is remarkable; what stays in the memory about Shera's experience is an extraordinary tale of doggie devotion. The starving mother and her large family were saved from certain death by a gentle labrador who recognised her fate.

Stealthily, day in and day out, he lifted cartons of milk from local doorsteps and conscientiously carried them over the golf course to desperate Shera. Was he the father of her puppies? Nobody knows, but I can tell you that they turned out to be healthy, happy young dogs, half labrador, half German Shepherd. So, you can draw your own conclusions.

Anxious about Shera's future, after reading the report, I phoned Mrs Tulloch for reassurance. She told me the dog was in poor condition; nervous and without trust. Already, however, she had found a foster-mother for some of the puppies — which was essential.

The intention, she said, was ultimately to find Shera a good home when her pups were weaned and when she, too, was well enough to go.

I asked to be kept informed about future developments and Sue did that. After all she had been through, I vowed, nothing was going to happen to Shera. If the worst came to the worst, I could perhaps...

At that time, Sue, inspired by the work of Kay Carmichael, of Peterculter, doyenne of dog rescue in the North-east, had only just become involved. Since then, she has had about 50 of that very handsome but much-maligned breed, the German Shepherd, through her hands.

Even now, she is still dismayed at the fickleness and fecklessness of some owners, who are willing to pay about £200 for a puppy and then want rid of it at the slightest irritation. In fact, any day now, many hundreds of dogs, Christmas presents whose novelty has worn off, will be cast out, abandoned or otherwise disposed of, throughout the country.

They tell her, these owners, that the dog is chasing sheep. Do they not know about discipline? They say the garden is in a mess. A good shovel does the job. Then there are hairs on the children's clothes. A good brush does not cost the earth.

Mostly, they are owners who find they cannot be bothered. Once, Sue found a seven-month-old puppy tied to her front door. At least its owners had taken the trouble to bring it to a place of safety. All too often, others cannot bestir themselves to do even that. Their pets are, quite simply, abandoned — on the motorway, in the country, somewhere, anywhere, as far away as possible.

Eventually, loving homes were found for Shera's puppies, but Bobby was kept to stop his mother — now gradually recovering her strength — from fretting. Then, in one phone call, Sue told me she had found a prospective owner for Shera; someone caring, someone experienced in German Shepherds, with four of her own. I could meet them both that week at a local canine-training class.

When I saw her, head hung low and still with that haunted look, Shera was thin and her coat was in poor condition. At every opportunity, she slunk under a form or under a table, out of sight. She trusted nobody.

For reasons that are not relevant, Shera did not go to the person who had four already. Instead, she was found a good and caring home with Liz Marshall and family, at Musselburgh, East Lothian, where she was the only dog.

After about a year there, Liz wrote to me to say: "When we first got her, Shera hid behind the couch for two months. She was terrified. Now she is a happy dog, eating anything and playing. She follows me everywhere and is becoming more secure day by day.

"She does lapse at times and reverts to being timid, but those times are fewer and fewer. She has come a long way, and we all love her."

That is the kind of ending I like best.

February 2, 1991

● *Shera continues to enjoy life with the kindly Marshall family at Musselburgh. Meanwhile, Sue and Robin Tulloch, who do so much to rescue and find homes for abandoned German Shepherds, have moved to Edelhof Kennels, at Easthaven, Carnoustie.*

FOR YOO–HOO!

FOR MORE than 30 years, I spent almost all of my holidays trying to get away from telephones. For all that time, the nature of the job was such that at least part of every day was spent on the phone. To be free from its strident summons was essential for any break.

So there is something ironic in the fact that no sooner had I retired from full-time work than I decided to invest in an answering machine.

I did not intend to spend my new-found leisure tied to the house lest the phone should ring. But did it really matter if I should lose a call or two while walking the dogs or pruning the roses? After all, there could be nothing too urgent, in these less-hurried days, and whoever-it-was could simply ring back.

But my mind was made up and whether the thing was essential or not had little to do with it. The fact is that, after all those years with one at my hand, I have become hooked on the phone. Now, at home, I could not bear not knowing who wanted to speak to me in my absence — or that nobody did.

Looking back, there were signs of potential addiction a long time ago.

Why was I so irritable, so impatient whenever it was out of order? Why did I not recognise these feelings of isolation, or restlessness, of being bereft — for the withdrawal symptoms they were?

If I had, I might have taken care to get in on the British Telecom share flotation and saved myself a pound or two. I do not use gas, nor am I a customer of the Bank That Likes To Say Yes, but I have shares in both of these and not in BT.

Like most addicts, I am reluctant to take the blame for my weakness. It must have started, surely, when, as a teenager, spending some time in England, I was encouraged to make a duty call home once a week.

In those days, the telephone system was a much more personal, friendly thing than now and I liked to hear the operators

making contact all the way up the line — York — Edinburgh
— Aberdeen. And, believe it or not, I got to know the
Aberdeen operator through those weekly calls.

"Do you think they'll accept reverse charges *again*?" he
would tease.

Nowadays, you're lucky if you can get hold of an operator,
let alone one who has time to chat. Which is probably just as
well, for the last thing I need is encouragement.

The new machine arrived, a smart, cream, box-like apparatus
with buttons which could do any number of tricks. All I wanted
it to do was to take messages when I was out and play them
back when I came in; a perfectly straightforward operation.

I set about taping the recorded message. Nothing elaborate,
you know, just the usual words: "This is Aberdeen xxxxxx. I
am sorry there is nobody here to take your call at the
moment..." And so on, and so on.

The first time one of my friends heard it, she had such a
shock that she dropped the receiver. "That was never you," she
complained later. "Didn't sound like you in the least. Not a bit
friendly."

Now, I admit I'm used to the written word and not to the spoken word, and I tend to be slightly inhibited by microphones.
But there was nothing for it except to try again. Make it sound
brisk and businesslike *and* warm and welcoming.

That's better. Now take the dogs for a walk. I returned an
hour or so later to find my robot winking knowingly, signalling
that a message was waiting. Go on, press the button. I do it gin-
gerly — and listen.

"Oh, just shut up!" spat an anonymous voice, rudely.

"Thanks a lot," I muttered, beginning to regret my latest
investment.

You see, I'm into gadgets. The problem is that they're usually
far too elaborate for my modest needs. One example is my cal-
culator, bought in a flush of optimism by one who once scored
half-a-mark in a school algebra exam for writing her name
neatly.

"Don't you think it's — er — maybe a bit too sophisticated?", my shopping companion suggested tentatively.

"You don't have to drive at 100 to enjoy a Jaguar," I snapped, "but it's nice to know the power is there."

Complicated or not, I do use my gadgets and I enjoy them, up to a point. That point comes when, in order to perform some more complex operation, I have to consult the manual. Someone once told me that all you needed to be able to cook well was to be able to read. I didn't agree then, and I don't agree now.

If that were true, all you would need to do in order to be able to drive would be to read the car's handbook. No, cookery books, like instruction manuals, tend to assume an altogether higher level of expertise or knowledge than a mere beginner generally has — which seems to be a mistake.

In any case, I have the utmost trouble with instruction books; in understanding them, I mean. What I need to get the best out of my equipment actually is to be shown what to do; a practical demonstration, in other words. And that usually isn't forthcoming in the shops these days.

The situation is bad enough when the instructions are in English, but can you imagine what it's like trying to follow a poor translation from the Japanese?

This is from the handbook of my Japanese off-road vehicle, explaining how to drive it in deep water:

"Before you enter the water, make sure to shift the transfer lever to the 4L position and also carefully check the conditions of water bottom."

At this very moment, I have before me the instructions for my latest "toy" and it's astonishing what it can do — if you know how. You can pretend to be out when you're in and listen to the voice before deciding whether or not to answer.

You can "save" your messages and play them back later if, for instance, you want someone else to hear them. And, incredibly, you can hear your messages from anywhere in the world simply by dialling your own number and using an access code.

But I intend to resist having a phone in the car or one of those models you can carry around with you, even in the garden.

Excuse me now; I must dash to answer the telephone.

It's for yoo-hoo!

July 9, 1988

BEAUTY QUEENS

THE whole point about having show dogs is to show them, they argued. To have show dogs and not to show them is rather like keeping an exquisite ornament out of sight in a drawer, isn't it?

Perhaps, but the truth is that I don't really care very much what other people think of my dogs. It's very pleasing, of course, if they happen to think, like me, that they're great. But not important.

What matters, in my opinion, is what I think of them and, to me, my dogs are the tops and there isn't a judge on the show circuit who could change my mind about that.

It really isn't disastrous, to my mind, if their eyes are a shade too pale by breed standard, or they're too long in the back or not deep enough in the chest. It would matter very much if I were a breeder because, presumably, those faults would be passed on.

But breeder I am not — and I'll tell you why. You see, I know me well enough to know that there is absolutely no way I could part with any of the progeny, not even one with bandy legs, flat feet and an undershot jaw. And that, realistically, could leave me with six or even eight more on top of my present two. No, as far as I am concerned, my dogs are pets, marvellous companions, first and foremost.

That's all very well, admiring friends persisted, but isn't it a little selfish? After all, if you do have a good dog, a fine example of its kind, don't you think you owe it to the breed to show it; to help keep up the standard?

To cut a long story short, I succumbed in the end, not without reservations and mainly because one of my friends who enjoys the show scene very much wanted to be allowed to show them.

First, though, I ought to tell you who "they" are. Regular readers of this column have been introduced already to Tess, the English setter I promised myself for many a long day. She's two now, but she was only one year old when it became increasingly obvious that she was desperate for a playmate. So Tansy arrived, a lovely tricolour puppy from the prominent kennel in Lancashire where Brenda Hacking produces such splendid setters, including two or three champions.

They're very different, as it happens, which makes them even more interesting. Tessa is affectionate, soft and kind, whereas Tansy is more intelligent, with a mind of her own and somewhat stand-offish. She'll pay you attention only when it suits, and then she'll throw her great, freckled arms around your neck and clutch you in a tight embrace.

Anyway, next month we're off on the dog-show circuit and I'll be there to see Tansy going through her paces. Soon, I will be able to tell the difference between championship shows, exemption shows, breed shows and bench shows. I have a great deal to learn. But, of course, it would be naïve to pretend that the world of dog-showing is just good fun. There is a lot of money involved, and this is indubitably the root of most of the trouble.

Thankfully, the horrid episodes we hear about, such as dogs being drugged, exhibitors threatened, of rampant jealousy, tend to occur in the South. I have yet to hear of any such thing happening in the North-east. In fact, it is precisely because of the kindness of English-setter people here that I have lost my initial reservations. People like Mrs May Cook, at Durris, who, despite having two or three lovely dogs of her own to prepare for a show, still found time to beautify mine.

And Mrs Sally Leiper, the Barbara Woodhouse of the North-east, who has forgotten more about dogs than most people know, on hand always to give sound and concerned advice.

However, for the rest of the season, Friday night will be Amami night at Maison Murray. Tansy actually enjoys all the beautification, clambering into the bath, holding her pretty face up to the spray and standing stock still while she is rubbed and blown dry.

Tess, on the other hand, thinks the whole thing is beneath her dignity. She seems to sense what is afoot and promptly vanishes. Then she has to be lifted bodily into the tub and persuaded to stay long enough for a decent shampoo. I have wished more than once that someone would breed a bald dog.

One advantage in a long-haired breed, apparently, is that the coat can be used, if necessary, to hide a fault, although that sort of trick is well beyond me. So is all the gamesmanship in the dog-show business. One breeder, an old hand at showing dogs, alerted me to one exhibitor well known, it seems, for gamesmanship. "Just wait until the turn of the rival dog and see what happens," he predicted.

Sure enough, just as the judge was examining the statuesque animal, the dog was startled by the metallic crash of a tin dog-dish dropped "accidentally" from a great height. I don't know if that kind of thing is permissible or not, but I thought it was carrying it much too far.

It's incredible, really, how much goes into it if you're going to take it seriously. The beauty treatment is just about the last step in a long process which stretches all the way back to the dog's earliest days.

It is only months old when it has its first lessons in ringcraft; learning how to behave in the showring; how to move well; to stand stock still; to allow the judge to feel it all over.

Then there are all those hours of road-walking to build up muscles. And the trimming must be done far enough ahead so that scissor marks will have grown out by the big day.

"If you don't win, it doesn't matter," one English-setter exhibitor once told me. "You're taking the same dog home."

I couldn't agree more.

July 30, 1988

LIFE ON ONE LEG

THE surgeon whose trousers I am wearing does not, I imagine, know I have them. But I would like him to know that, over the past 10 days, they have helped to make bearable life on one leg.

The pale-green theatre trousers are hardly the height of sartorial elegance, but they are lightweight and cool and easy to wear. They were given me by a resourceful nurse who, having dressed my injured leg, then discovered I had no apparel wide enough to accommodate the enormous bandage.

That young nurse will go a long way. There I was, immobile, incarcerated in my underwear in the accident and emergency unit of Aberdeen Royal Infirmary, with nothing to wear on the way home. It did not take her a second to "purloin" the trousers and lend them to me — courtesy of the National Health Service.

What happened? You might well ask. It was the first question they asked when, shaken and in pain, I put myself at their mercy. It is an unlikely tale.

"You'll never believe it," I told the male nurse who took my notes when I arrived.

"Try me," he coaxed.

Outside, a woman, herself on crutches, could hardly bear to watch as I eased myself laboriously out of the car. As she waited for a taxi, she grabbed a nearby wheelchair and helped to ease me into it.

When I turned to thank her, she had gone.

Inside, patients sat in rows, chatting with companions, flicking through magazines, waiting to be seen. They sported an assortment of aids, from various kinds of sticks to crutches, full-length and elbow-length.

Nurses in colourful shoulder tabs came and went, their white shoes squeaking on shiny floors. Their presence was soothing and reassuring and gave me confidence.

I could not speak for the others but, for myself, I was greatly relieved to be there after a short journey which, nevertheless, seemed to hurt every inch of the way.

The male nurse was intent. "What happened?" he repeated.

"You won't believe it," I said, "but one step of our stairs gave way and I fell all the way down."

Unlikely — because you don't expect the tread of a stair to vanish beneath your feet. Not any old stair, mind you, but a trendy, sturdy, open-tread one, designed by an architect.

"The doctor will be with you in a minute," said the male nurse, putting away his pen and vanishing behind the yellow curtains.

The doctor arrived promptly, young and confident and full of Irish charm. No, there were no fractures. Yes, they would have it X-rayed. Keep the weight off it. Rest the knee. No problems. All in a day's work.

I was wheeled away, not cursing my misfortune but grateful for my good luck that all I had were sprained ligaments when it could have been a broken neck or a damaged spine.

Half an hour later, I left on crutches, wearing the surgeon's trousers and clutching a few painkillers, to begin convalescence as one of the walking wounded, thinking that the emergency staff could have been hand-picked for their endless job at the sharp end of their profession.

In fact, it was my second visit to Aberdeen's splendid accident and emergency unit. Not long after it opened, I was given an all-night assignment to describe how the emergency team repaired human debris after a Saturday night on the city's wild side.

As someone who makes a detour of miles rather than pass a road accident, frankly, I had been dreading it. But that night I learned that blood and gore are not necessarily the accompaniments to danger; that destiny can creep up silently and unexpectedly and with a peaceful face.

Back home, I mastered my crutches and was soon hopping around on them, up and down stairs, laboriously out and in. Then I became quite adept at taking all the weight on my good leg, merely balancing with the other — a procedure, I suspect, which might not be recommended.

"You should sue the architect," a friend exploded when I

described my accident and, in those first days, I was sorely tempted — and I mean that, literally. Of course, I have not and will not, for I fail to see what good that would do. The fault, it appears, was one of design and not of workmanship, so it was the architect's responsibility.

I have graduated from full-length crutches to elbow-crutches, to a couple of sticks and there is progress.

Having been so restricted in my own mobility over the past week or so has given me an insight into what many people have to cope with in a permanent way.

One good thing to come out of my small misadventure is an even greater regard for those who endure some of life's worst vicissitudes with cheerfulness — and somehow manage to enhance life for others.

That, I think, takes smeddum.

August 18, 1990

REYNARD

I T IS a long time since I rose willingly with the dawn. In fact, it is so long ago now that I can't remember when, although I imagine it must have been to make a good start for a day in the hills, when getting up with the lark did not seem like hardship.

There are, of course, times when early rising is unavoidable. Like going to the airport to catch the first flight or driving visitors to the station for a dawn departure. But that is different, done because it has to be done and not out of choice. The other week, however, I left my warm bed in the early morning, not reluctantly but eagerly.

The last of the snow clung to the dykes around the field in front of the house and, beyond that, on a piece of rough ground thick with bracken and gorse, trees stirred in the watery light.

Shivering, I scanned the wintry landscape for a sight of him, peering through binoculars wherever a movement caught my eye. Would he show up —or not? You see, we did not have an assignation which, like a tryst, is an arrangement between two parties.

Indeed, I have to say that the attraction was not mutual, that if he knew I was there he would not come at all. There's no fool like an old ...

Then, suddenly, there he was in the corner of the field. Entranced, I watched him, his handsome head held high as he stood motionless, surveying the scene, before leaping lithely over the dyke and into the thicket. I am sure he was the same fox which first aroused my interest in him and his kind.

My romance with Reynard began in the autumn when there, on that same dyke, I first saw him perched with his partner, the pair, cat-like, licking their whiskers, presumably after a meal. Intrigued, I told neighbours and friends and anyone else who would listen about the exciting sighting. And almost everyone had a tale to tell about those magnificent, wild creatures who inhabit our countryside.

One friend confided reverently that the fox gets rid of his fleas by swimming, balancing a ball of wool above the surface. The drowning fleas crowd on to the wool in an attempt to save their lives, leaving the fox flea-free. Such, she said, is their cunning.

Several spoke about people finding all the chickens in a run slaughtered by a fox who had killed for the sake of it, because he could not have eaten them all. And I have often heard farmers complain about losing some lambs in night raids by Reynard. Such is his savagery.

Few animals, it seems, divide opinion so much — you either love him or loathe him. You are likely to love him if, like me, you like to watch him in the wild; to hate him if, like farmers or landowners, you believe he kills your lambs or your chickens, your grouse and pheasants.

And such a mythology has grown up around him, especially about his cruel capacity for killing, that it is difficult to tell which tales are true and which are not.

All this served to heighten my curiosity and I mentioned it to Johnny, the trapper, next time I came across him as I walked my dogs in the woods. He spoke of Reynard in tones which bordered on awe. Aye, he confirmed, there are lots of them around, more than ever, and he guessed there could be twenty families of them in the mere 10 miles between Maryculter and Aberdeen.

I needed to speak to an expert and the man was Dick Balharry, the knowledgeable chief warden of the Nature Conservancy Council in the North-east. Dick admits not just to a respect but to a love for the fox.

"They are magnificent animals and very, very timid," he enthused. "Their chief enemy is man, but they are very unlikely to attack unless they are threatened. I realise, though, that they come into conflict with man's needs and there must be some control."

Their numbers are increasing, he said, because there are more young woodlands where they find food and shelter and because there are fewer gamekeepers. They are increasing in urban areas, too, where they are especially hard to control.

Dick told me where they live — in enlarged rabbit burrows,

in stone cairns, or in sandholes; what they eat — rabbit and voles, rats and mice, carrion, ground-nesting birds such as grouse and pheasant and the occasional lamb.

He told me how to track them — distinctive pad marks about a foot apart, and in almost a straight line, five pads at the front, four at the back, and how to know when they're around — by their unique, pungent smell after you get to know it; by their tapered droppings which contain dry matter like deer or rabbit hair and the small bones of little creatures.

They mated for life and were faithful until death, said Dick, who also insisted that their reputation for killing lambs was greatly exaggerated. They took only an occasional lamb to feed their cubs, generally born about the end of March.

But farmer Derry Argue called from Tain to tell me a different story. Not only did they kill lambs, he said, but they also savaged sheep which were in some way disabled. He had seen the evidence himself — and he went on to describe in gory detail their wicked ways of death.

Dr Ray Hewson, of the Institute of Terrestial Ecology at Banchory, has made a couple of academic studies of foxes and he was sceptical, on the whole, about their killing of grown sheep, even if incapacitated.

No matter. That night, I thought about the little lambs with their bright coats who fill the spring with their tender noise. Man is no better than fox in their fate and I considered a vegetarian future.

This — without getting round to explaining why — I was busy telling a friend on the phone a few days later. It was about noon, in fact, on a fine day last week. The snow no longer lay along the dykes and, as we talked, I was looking out over the field, its ploughed furrows straight and rich and dark. When, suddenly, my eye caught a movement along the top dykeside.

"Here is Reynard!" I cried, putting down the receiver. "I'll ring you back."

Fascinating as ever, he was, as he stalked along the wall and then, as I watched, he pounced, all four feet together, in an elegant death dance ...

March 19, 1988

EMMA'S DAY

T HERE cannot be much in life to surpass the sharing of a special moment with family or friends or someone very dear. The sort of thing I have in mind takes a great deal more than money — not a posh party, a gourmet dinner, an exotic holiday or anything like that. These can be bought.

I was thinking, rather, of those particular moments of celebration which are beyond price, which all the money in the world cannot buy and which are especially precious for that very reason. Thoughts like these swirled around in my mind as, last week, the early-morning train sped south to Edinburgh.

There is not much nowadays, I have to say, which will get me out of bed cheerfully at 6 a.m., but this had the promise of a happy day, one which would sparkle forever in the memory — a day we had long anticipated and one which would crown youthful endeavour with deserved success.

I was on my way to watch my god-daughter, Emma, graduate from Edinburgh University with an honours degree in politics at a ceremony in the capital's imposing McEwan Hall. And even BR, apparently sensing the day's pre-eminence, for once obliged in being fast, efficient — and on time.

The taxi driver at Waverley Station was different. "The McEwan Hall?" he queried, puzzled.

"Yes," I confirmed, "where today's graduation is taking place."

"There have been graduations all over the city this week," he countered and, getting out, he asked for directions from a colleague in the taxi rank behind.

As we sped through the Edinburgh traffic, I resisted the temptation to point out that, if he did not know where the McEwan Hall was, he jolly well should. Surely the whole point of taking a cab is that one is lifted easily from one point and deposited exactly at another, without hassle. But our man drew in at the kerb of a busy thoroughfare and grinned an apology. "It's somewhere round here," he said.

Shrugging off this minor irritation, I was by now preparing myself for an element of anticlimax. I was, after all, not going to be seeing anything new: this was the last of my three god-daughters to graduate and I had been at every ceremony — and that in this generation, alone.

We followed a couple of young men, their black gowns worn over kilts, to the hall where, in front, parents and friends in floppy hats and Sunday suits waited for the doors to open.

Inside, the booming notes of the organ echo to the domed roof and the seats at the front are filling up with graduands. Their silk hoods of white, green, maroon and gold, pale blue and yellow carpet the floor with colour, like so many multi-coloured blooms in a great garden.

Tomorrow's vets, teachers, journalists and many others are jubilant, laughing, talking among themselves, turning occa-sionally to wave to proud relatives or friends in the gallery. As we wait for the "capping" to begin, I wonder how many know anything of the symbolism or significance of the ceremony we are about to watch.

In mediaeval times, universities were basically guilds or asso-ciations of Masters, and the degree of MA was the step to full membership. In fact, the act of "capping" is an imitation of the old Roman practice of manumission, when a cap was placed on the head of the emancipated slave. Thus, the cap became the symbol of the liberation of the graduand from restrictive disci-pline, guidance and instruction.

The academic dress — the gown, hood and trencher (some-times called a mortarboard) — also recalls the ancient universi-ties' lineage as relics of mediaeval clerical costume for, in ori-gin, the ceremony is ecclesiastical. Originally, the hood had a practical use to cover the head. Now, in its shape and the colour of its silk lining, it is the distinctive mark of a particular degree and university.

The ceremony varies only in small detail from university to university. We missed, for instance, the rousing chorus of "Gaudeamus" and the sonorous Latin which so dignifies the Aberdeen graduation, but we liked the formal white tie worn by the young men with their academic dress in Edinburgh.

Now they are stepping up one by one to the dais, to be

Chatting with the Queen Mother on a visit to Aberdeen Journals in 1972. I was features editor of the Press and Journal at the time.

My brother, Kenny, a well-known Highland League footballer in the 1950s.

My god-daughter, Emma Simpson, with her mother on graduation day, 1990. See P49.

touched on the head by the vice-chancellor. All 450 of them; one every five seconds. We applaud them all and the proceedings advance on a surge of emotion. At last, she steps up, young and smiling. It is a picture we will store forever in the memory.

"Well done, Emma," we whisper audibly and, all unwittingly, we clap louder and longer than the rest. There is the unexpected lump in the throat, the compelling mix of pride and thankfulness, joy and hope. It has not changed at all.

There was food for thought in vice-chancellor Sir David Smith's address. He lamented the fact that British universities were still predominantly middle-class institutions, and he wondered how more people from disadvantaged sectors could be recruited when the personal financial position of university students is deteriorating.

In a reference to the introduction of student loans, the imminent freezing of maintenance grants, the withdrawal of housing benefit and liability for the poll tax, Sir David asked how under-privileged people could be attracted to become students living in debt, instead of going from school into paid jobs.

The injustice of that preoccupied us on the way home. It will preoccupy us until it is set to rights. But, for that day, it was not allowed to cloud an occasion which was joyous and optimistic and which did the heart good.

Gaudeamus igitur.

July 21, 1990

● *Emma is the daughter of my old friend and colleague, Ethel Simpson, the doyenne of a former generation of North-east reporters. Emma followed her mother into journalism and, as a reporter with Scottish Television, she is beamed regularly into sitting-rooms in Central Scotland.*

Mums' Army

MY EARLIEST memory of "the Rural" is of a dark night in the wartime winter of either 1941 or 1942. For weeks, two of our household had been practising for their parts in the local institute's annual concert and we children were to be in the audience.

At that time our home was at Lonmay, in a quiet rural area between Peterhead and Fraserburgh — not on the coast, but not far from it, on the tip of what, in those war-torn days, was known as "Hellfire Corner".

The soubriquet arose from the aerial dogfights which exploded regularly in local skies, shattering the peace as RAF pilots defended our northbound convoys under attack by Nazi airmen.

The night of the concert duly came, black as pitch, and we fidgeted as, scrubbed and polished, we waited for the hired car to arrive which would take us to the local hall. It was John Findlay's taxi from the nearby Ban-Car Hotel.

The country road was barely discernible in the faint beam of masked headlights as we were driven the two or so miles there. And we had almost arrived when, suddenly, the staccato rasp of gunfire tore the air above us and bullets traced gossamer patterns in the sky.

There was, I remember, no hint of fear or anxiety in the car and certainly no question of turning back; in retrospect, I wonder how much effort and self-control had gone into that show of calm.

Outside, shadowy figures scurried around in the blackout, hurrying to get into the hall's shelter and, inside, all was light and bright as the music played and the concert began. We joined in rousing choruses of such classics as The White Cliffs of Dover and Run, Rabbit, Run, despite intermittent competition from choirs of screaming bullets above us. By the time we rose to sing the National Anthem, the dogfight was done.

Throughout World War II, the redoubtable ranks of SWRI

women knitted comforts for the troops, helped organise evacuees, made-do-and-mended and distributed cod-liver oil and ration books.

They did many other things besides, but never, I am sure, did a bunch of Rural women anywhere disport themselves more bravely than they did that night. They were not about to let anyone as insignificant as Adolf Hitler spoil their fun.

The respect and admiration I have for the Scottish Women's Rural Institutes was born that night so long ago.

Now, half a century on, the SWRI is coming to the end of a year of celebrations to mark its 75th birthday. Celebrations will cease at the conclusion of the national handicrafts and house-wives conference and exhibition to be held in Aberdeen in September.

When that is over, the 75th-jubilee flag — having been trooped proudly round the country with great ceremony for the past 12 months — will be lowered finally and taken to Balmoral Castle by a small group of national delegates who have been invited to take tea with the Queen.

The junketing has taken many forms, for the women of "the Rural" are good at fun. The idea that I liked best was that of all 1,116 Scottish institutes having a simultaneous tea party on June 7, either indoors or outdoors, making, I imagine, the biggest tea party of all time.

Some climbed Bennachie, I am told, and others Tap o' Noth. Maud, Cairnbanno and New Deer came together in Maud Hall for a Taste 'n' Try. At Birkenhills, near Turriff, they opted for a good, old-fashioned picnic.

The date was chosen to coincide with the setting out from East Lothian — where Scotland's first institute was formed at Longniddry in June, 1917 — of the jubilee flag at the start of its trail. Its subsequent arrival in each of the 34 federations will be an occasion for a get-together of members and it is expected in Aberdeenshire next month, ultimately to be taken to Alford, where Aberdeenshire's first institute was set up in 1918.

Strangely enough, it was a death that gave rise to the birth of this formidable regiment of women in Canada in 1897. Farmer's wife Mrs Hoodless mourned the death of her son and cursed her own ignorance in feeding him contaminated milk.

More than 100 women turned up for the meeting she called at Stoney Creek and that same night the movement was formed with the aims and objects just as they are today: to provide social, educational and recreational opportunities for country-women or those interested in country life.

In the early years, the SWRI provided a haven of warmth, companionship, instruction and fun for countrywomen whose lives were too often full of hard work, isolation and loneliness. The monthly meeting was perhaps their only night out in four weeks, something to be eagerly anticipated and enjoyed to the full.

Over the years, the Rural adapted to meet the demands of a changing world without losing sight of its fundamental purpose. From pancakes and scones and jam-makers par excellence, it progressed to more sophisticated images of speech-makers, golfers, musicians and photographers, who still had time for more traditional skills.

Now, on its 75th birthday, it has come to another crossroads. The problem is falling membership due largely to the loss of jobs in the countryside.

In 1976, the SWRI had 54,000 members compared with 37,000 today, and Aberdeenshire, still the biggest federation, with 3,500, has shed 1,500 members in 12 years. It is greatly to be hoped it will survive and go on for the benefit of future generations of countrywomen.

That is why, with special feeling, I wish it Many Happy Returns.

July 18, 1992

GHOST STORIES

TWO items appeared on the same day in the newspapers last week which reminded me again of the truth of the English Bard's remark about there being more things in heaven and earth than we can dream of ... even now.

The first was a report of mysterious orange balls spotted over Aberdeen, late at night. The UFOs were said to have been heading in a northerly direction at only a few hundred feet up.

Motorists in the city's Queens Road were reported to have stopped their vehicles to join pedestrians gazing skywards at the strange objects which, according to an eyewitness, were travelling at incredible speed.

The other item was about the sale of an elegant, former manse near Alford, Aberdeenshire. It is a Category B listed property, once lived in by the Reverend James Duncan, known for his involvement in compiling the Greig-Duncan Folk Song Collection.

The story, however, had more to do with the fact that the property is said to be haunted by a naked man, a benevolent spectre, seen by all three of the present family. There was "nothing sinister" about the ghost, one of the owners is quoted as saying. "It is a very happy, warm and friendly house."

Not having had any definite, personal experience, I can only keep an open mind about ghosts and the supernatural, but I cannot say the same about UFOs.

On a pitch-black autumn evening about 15 years ago, I was driving home towards Aberdeen with a friend after a political meeting at Banchory. It must have been about 10.30pm and we had driven only a few miles towards the city on the North Deeside Road to a point where the road is straight and fringed with trees.

Suddenly, coming towards us at great speed between the trees, was a large circle of bright light. It passed low over the car and, over my shoulder, I could see it land in the adjoining field, just a large circle of dazzling brilliance.

We were very frightened and, safe at home discussing the sighting, we wondered if any others had seen it; if anything would be reported next day. Nothing was.

What was it? A flying-saucer manned by extraterrestrial crew? A shooting star falling harmlessly to earth? A meteorite? I shall never know. What I remember still is the eerie silence of the thing and telling my colleagues in the office next day about my experience.

"Did you not take enough water in it, then?" they chided.

Given that sort of reaction, it is not surprising that people who do have paranormal experiences are reluctant, very often, to talk about them.

Because I know them as people very well, I am convinced that what happened separately to two of my friends was exactly as they described it.

Sam is as stolid, practical and honest as any of his Buchan breed and I knew him quite a long time before he told me about the night when — his deliveries complete — he was driving home one winter in a storm. It was "blin' drift", as they say in that part of the world, and Sam was almost upon the old woman before he knew it, her bent figure caught in the lights of the van as she plodded through the snow by the woods at Bonnykelly.

He pulled up wondering, as he jumped down from the van, what an aul' body was doing out in such a night. She agreed to a lift and he helped her into the passenger seat, placing her little case at her feet. He climbed in himself, started the van, turned to speak to his passenger. But her seat was empty.

Alice, a friend of many years, is now a widow and living in England. She had been very preoccupied with plans for her daughter's wedding, coping with many of the arrangements on her own. Her late husband had been much in her mind and, especially at that time, she was missing his support.

One morning, before the wedding, she awoke with a start, aware of a presence at the end of her bed. At first, she was very frightened, but she recognised her husband as he moved towards her.

"Do you approve of everything?" she asked him at last.

He smiled, nodded — and was gone.

Neither Sam nor Alice are keen to speak openly about their experiences, almost, somehow, as if they had something to be ashamed of. I have news for them. They are in good company, for even the Queen is said to have seen a ghost.

According to a recent book by Peter Underwood, one of Britain's leading authorities on the paranormal, the kilted figure of John Brown is often seen stalking the corridors and the entrance hall at Balmoral.

It was there, in the entrance hall to the castle about 10 years ago, that Her Majesty is reported to have seen the ghost of Queen Victoria's faithful ghillie.

The Queen Mother, too, who spent her childhood in one of Scotland's most haunted castles, can be no stranger to the supernatural. Indeed, her younger brother, the late Sir David Bowes-Lyon, was said to have "the gift".

When their elder brother, Michael, an officer in World War I, was reported killed in action, the family at Glamis were plunged into grief. But David refused to mourn, insisting that his brother was still alive; that he had "seen" him twice; that he was in a large house surrounded by many trees, and that he had a bandage round his head.

David was proved right. News came through to Glamis several months afterwards that the eldest son had been wounded in the head and was in a German PoW hospital.

As for me…?

Apart from the Deeside UFO, my only experience of the paranormal is on the written page. Vivid memories remain of adolescence when I would take a book of ghost stories to bed, read until the early hours and scare myself witless, too paralysed even to put out the light.

May 14, 1988

HAPPY TO MEET

A GREAT many of you out there, it seems, appear to have the notion that it is always the bad news which makes the headlines — never the good. I can understand why. By its very nature, "news" comprises what is different or bizarre; what is out of the ordinary. And it seems to me that, as long as that is the case; as long as news is out of the everyday run, that can be no bad thing.

It would be a dreadful world, would it not, if the good news was considered so rare as to merit headline treatment?

What brought all this to mind was something which happened to me a few weeks ago and which, in its own way, gives the lie to any idea that it is exclusively the bad and the wrongdoing which hog the headlines.

I had no way of knowing when I set out that day what was to transpire. My destination was Esslemont House, near Ellon, where Mrs Rosemary Wolrige Gordon was holding an Open Day under Scotland's Gardens Scheme, of which she is joint organiser in Grampian Region.

Now I happen to believe that there cannot be many more pleasant or relaxing ways to while away a summer afternoon than by strolling round an interesting garden at one's leisure.

It is not simply the gardener's wondrous work, the landscaping, the juxtaposition of colour and plants, the ideas one can find for one's own, humbler plot. At Esslemont, it can be all these things.

For me, there is something more. The beauty of the setting, the unhurried calm, the obvious order, the sense that, in it all, there is a higher hand, tend to foster a deep satisfaction and an inner content.

In this, I suspect I am far from alone. In Grampian, we are fortunate, for every year there are about 19 splendid gardens to see (of cottage, as well as of castle, some grand and formal, others intimate and small), under the Gardens Scheme, with the proceeds going to charity.

In fact, last year, about £10,000 was raised in Grampian alone for a host of deserving causes – thanks to the garden owners, who seem positively to welcome in all the world and his wife to tramp over their well-tended turf.

By the time I arrived, the sun had brought out a good crowd to boost an event rapidly becoming one which is looked forward to by Buchan folk as a grand day out. People in casual clothes strolled around, looking at the gardens, visiting the charity stands, trying their hand at tombola, listening to the Ythan Fiddlers and exchanging gossip with acquaintances they met.

I had barely left the car park when I was told that there had been a call for me over the public-address system. It transpired that a stranger wanted to see me, a woman who would not give her name or business.

The mystery deepened...

In the course of the day, I had forgotten all about it when a smiling, middle-aged woman approached, her hand outstretched, and she introduced herself simply as Mrs Smith from Pitcaple. I had never met her before.

"I wanted to thank you," she began, "for putting me in touch with the sister I never knew."

As she spoke, I was transported in time and place from the quiet of a country-house garden to the terror and turmoil of an air raid over Fraserburgh. That raid and, in particular, its tragic consequences for one woman, was the subject of one of a series of features I wrote in 1987.

It was based on readers' memories of World War II, and one of those who responded, Mrs Smith was telling me, was Mrs Isabella McIntosh, from Stonehaven, whose maiden name was Reid. Isabella's mother had been killed in the Fraserburgh raid that tragic day in March, 1941, after having cycled from her home at nearby Memsie to the town on an errand.

The story was told in print and I had a phone call subsequently from a woman reader who, from the details, suspected strongly that Isabella was the half-sister she had never known. That woman was the grateful reader standing talking to me now in the middle of all the activity at Esslemont.

Mrs Barbara Smith told me that she was there especially to

say "thank you" for putting them in touch. Soon afterwards, over tea with Babs Smith at her home at Pitcaple, she tried to convey how much happiness and pleasure her new-found half-sister had brought into the lives of herself, her husband, Gordon, and their daughter, Angela.

"My late father had spoken so much about Sybil that I wanted to meet her," Mrs Smith said. "I had heard she lived in the Stonehaven area, but I didn't want to go looking. I didn't want to intrude. Then, when, I saw the bit in the newspaper, I knew it was her.

"I phoned you and asked you to tell her to get in touch. You did and, soon afterwards, we went down to see her at Stonehaven. I had not seen her for 40 years. You see, I am the elder one of my father's second family and I wasn't very old when Sybil left home in her teens.

"In any case, I just wept when we met. She was so like my father. We visit often and I cannot tell you how much her friendship means to us all.

"It was just meant to be, our meeting. That's all I can say."

The little sequel to a story long forgotten by me crowned a happy day at Ellon.

What was that about newspapers never printing good news?

September 14, 1991

THE LAST TIME...

THE last time I saw her, she was sitting by the fire with a travelling-rug thrown loosely around her shoulders. It was, I think, the rug which brought it home to me: the fact that she needed it; the realisation that she was growing old.

She who had been so much part of our youth; who, through all the years, had always been there. She who had kept an open door and an open mind, especially for those in trouble or need.

Life without her seemed unimaginable.

It was not so much what she said or did, although her understanding was real and her empathy obvious. It was, rather, the fact that she was there, always there, steadfast as a rock and loyal to a fault.

She was not physically strong. She looked frail, sitting there, years of suffering etched on her face. Yet the lovely hair was thick and wavy still, greying only slightly at the temples.

But what she lacked in physical strength she had in other ways. Paradoxically, her remarkable strength of character seemed to grow out of years of suffering and ill-health. "You're just as old as you feel," she said reassuringly that day. But she looked me straight in the eye and I knew she knew what was in my mind.

As was her wont, she turned the conversation deftly from her to me — how I was, what I had been doing, what plans I had, what I thought about this and that. One measure of that strength was to deflect any concern about her by focusing, with a genuine interest, on others.

I told her what I had been doing, who I had seen, what they had said. That way, part of the outside world came into her living-room, for she had been unable to be out for many weeks.

Long days were circumscribed by the postman's knock, the ice-cream bell, the scaling school, a neighbour gardening, another shopping, someone waving as they passed the window.

The view was over the roofs of the rest of the village, out over the river and away to the horizon where, beyond it to the south, lay the city of Aberdeen. Not much of a city woman was she. Her life had been bounded by her beloved Buchan, where she grew up, married, had her children and saw every one of her grandchildren safely into the world.

She would not have had it any other way.

My mind went back to my first memory of her.

No more than three or four, I was wheeled out for an afternoon stroll by her and one of her girlfriends, out of the village, up the brae, through the woods and past where soon a prisoner-of-war camp would appear.

Young as I was, I remember that clearly. From that day on, she seemed never far from the centre of our lives — caring, encouraging, guiding and never forgetting to praise when she thought praise was due.

Those early days were full of music and song, for she loved to sing and play the piano. Once, confined to bed during a long and difficult convalescence, she taught herelf to play the violin with the help of only a do-it-yourself manual.

Thrilled, we used to listen to her voice in the church choir, soaring and sweet, and, on Sunday afternoons, she would lead a sing-song round the piano in what was then called the parlour, a rather grand name for what it was.

In those pre-war days, we children were forbidden to play or prank in the parks or in the streets on Sundays. It was always Sunday best — to me, that was hairy stockings and stiff, tight shoes — and a sedate walk after church.

Little wonder those musical interludes were such a joy, breaking, as they did, the crushing monotony of Sabbath inactivity. The songs we sang were not, surprisingly, the popular numbers of the day. Those were not, on the whole, her taste. That was more for oratorio, operetta or for old ballads, some of them Victorian. She would play and sing and we learned them all at her knee.

To this day, I cannot hear I'll Walk Beside You or The Kerry Dancers and more without — with a stab — her memory flooding back.

At last, the day drew nigh to which she had been looking forward so much — and never could there have been a more grudging flower-girl than I. We children disliked the thought that this new man in our lives would take her away. He did, but not far, although to us it could have been the other side of the moon.

We need not have worried. She made sure that, on prolonged holidays, we saw as much of her as ever. We even grew to love the man, our new Uncle Donald, who had taken her away. And, on those happy wartime holidays, they planned treasure-hunts in the garden with trinkets hidden in trees; played hide-and-seek round the hayricks and sang the old familiar songs round the piano in the farmhouse at Mains of Annochie, Auchnagatt.

When her own children came, it was no different. We were involved with them from the start.

The last time I saw her, she came to the door to see me off, waving until the car was out of sight. It was with a leaden heart that I drove home, sensing, sadly, the beginning of the end.

And so it proved.

She died 12 years ago this week: my special aunt, my best friend. It seems like yesterday and it seems like a lifetime. But she lives on through her example of courage, endurance and kindness. The most extraordinary "ordinary" woman I have ever known.

March 6, 1993

Party Piece

THE LEAST we can do for those public-spirited men and women standing for election in our regional councils is to go out and vote. We owe it to them but, just as important, we owe it to ourselves.

I cannot understand why it is that general elections tend to generate near-hysteria when apathy seems all that surrounds them in local government. If national politics is a dirty game, in local government it must be discouraging and thankless.

The first general election I can remember was in 1945 and, since then, politics has fascinated me. At that time, the voting age was 21 and I, barely a teenager, had no vote. In fact, my total contribution the first time was to festoon the family car with placards and posters, ready for its function of ferrying voters to the polls.

The reason I remember the 1945 contest so well is something else. We children knew Winston Churchill from our parents and teachers as a great war leader who helped us to victory, saved us from Nazis and delivered us from all sorts of evil.

In that first post-war election, the Conservatives campaigned on the slogan: "Let Churchill finish the job", while the Labour Party launched a strong programme of social and economic reform.

Our young minds did not grasp the fact that there might be a difference between what it takes to be a great warrior and a great peacetime leader. Nor did it occur to us that the British people would not want Churchill, their national hero. But reject him they did.

Listening to the final results on the radio in an ice-cream café during lunch-break, my classmates and I learned the will of the people.

For the benefit of those who are too young to remember, Clement Attlee was returned for the Labour Party with a majority of 146 and the socialists became the majority party for the first time in their history.

The implications of all this we were too callow to calculate, but we were not too young to feel an empathy with the old warrior in his humiliation. I can recall distinctly a sense of disillusion, a mistrust, a questioning. What sort of people were they who so lately lionised him and now so callously cast him off? And what kind of a dirty game was politics?

I had my first sharp lesson then in what politics can be about.

Is something similar not happening to Margaret Thatcher today? You don't have to approve of everything she has done — of even anything she has done — to find distasteful the shameful, personal attacks now showered upon her.

The point is not that she is being taken to task. That, of course, is the democratic right of political commentators, of her opponents and even of colleagues of her own persuasion, if they think fit.

No, the objection is about the scurrilous nature of it. Bad enough when it comes from the opposite side, but caddish and thoroughly disloyal when it emanates from "friends" of her own hue. Did nobody ever tell them that it was never sound strategy to shoot the captain in the midst of the battle? Counterproductive, too, I should think, because this sort of behaviour offends a sense of decency which cuts across party lines.

It strikes me, watching the televised proceedings in the House of Commons, that there is not much wit around these days. Wit in a politician — or, indeed, in any public speaker — can be a wonderful weapon, and the late Lord Boothby had it in abundance.

As a schoolgirl, I was fortunate enough to meet Bob Boothby at home; to listen in our own sitting-room to him pontificating about politics — he of the great, booming voice, the silver tongue, the charismatic presence.

Not long after that, he addressed a political meeting in our local hall. What was the essence of his speech I can no longer remember.

But when it came to question time, someone in the audience asked something about beef imports from the Argentine. Boothby answered eloquently and at length.

Then a clergyman in the audience stood up. "Have you ever been to the Argentine, Mr Boothby?" he inquired.

"No."

"Then what makes you think you can talk about it so intimately?"

The Member for East Aberdeenshire drew himself up to his imposing height. "Sir," he began, "have you ever been to Heaven — or hell? Then what makes you think you are qualified to speak about either?"

His last words were drowned in laughter and applause as the minister, shaking his head, shrank into his seat.

Later, working as a young reporter, the grinding urban poverty I saw in city slums and tenements had a personal impact and my politics took a radical turn.

I had, of course, seen rural deprivation before, but somehow it never quite seemed so bad. There was always an old hen for the pot or something nutritional growing about the place for those who were hungry.

In any case, I became a political activist for a while and canvassed in more than one general election. It was, of course, a serious enterprise, a trade with its own tricks, but there were lighter moments, too. I remember staying up all night, mixing flour and water in the kitchen to make paste for political posters being erected under cover of darkness — hardly a cerebral exercise, but a job which had to be done.

I recall, aiming for a 100% canvass of a scattered rural area, driving up a long and pitted farm road to reach a single voter in the cottage at its end. The elderly woman kept us chatting, asking question upon question, leading us to believe our candidate had her vote.

She saw us to the door. "Noo," she said at last, "it's gey late. Ye winna get roon mony mair the nicht." By keeping us there, she had ensured that we would not.

My view is that it is wrong that party politics has any part in local government, but most of the candidates in the forthcoming regional contests are standing under party colours. They are all, we must assume, men and women who are prepared to put service before self in the highest tradition of public life.

One of them deserves your vote.

April 28, 1990

LOADSAMONEY

THE fact that I had never been to a top football game in my life seemed to matter not in the least. Neither did the shameful situation of never having seen the Dons play — although supporting them from a distance — appear to matter, either.

Admittedly, I had often watched Highland League matches when my brother, Kenny, played centre-forward for Fraserburgh FC, and later for Deveronvale. That, however, was long ago and, even then, I knew nothing of the subtleties of the game.

But knowing little about football might even be an advantage, they said. "Go on," they urged. "Someone's got to win and it could just as well be you."

So this season I took to doing the pools. Now, I am not, in any game of chance, one of life's winners. We all know someone whose name comes up regularly in the office sweep or Christmas raffle. I am not one of them.

For years, I was one of an office syndicate which had a few small wins but nothing really worthy of mention. Until then, the only other item I had won was a tin of boot polish many years ago at a sale of work. It was delivered to me personally at a cost in time and trouble of more than the whole thing was worth.

For some reason which escapes me now, I did try the pools in the late 1980s. And so keyed up was I at the prospect of a fortune that weeks went by when my coupon was not even checked!

One morning during this time, I was going through the post before setting off to work. Hurriedly, I tossed a brightly coloured envelope from the pools people into the waste-paper bin, half-opened, thinking it was just another piece of junk mail.

But there was something about a corner of the contents which looked suspiciously like a cheque, and this drew me up. I retrieved the torn envelope and extricated a cheque for more than £400 — my first pools win of any consequence.

The memory of that had, I am sure, something to do with my decision to try the pools again with a standing entry of 12 numbers. Once again, the pools excited me not and I lapsed back into failing even to check my coupon.

"I suppose you haven't checked your coupon?" came the question as I prepared to go out one Sunday afternoon. I shook my head and left.

"I don't want to raise your hopes," I was told when I returned, "but I think you might have won something on the pools. I make it that you have 23 points. My guess is that your score would qualify for a second dividend. That could be as much as half a million, maybe more."

I shook my head in disbelief.

As it happens, I have never tended to indulge in fantasies about what I would do with a big pools win. To me, that seemed the ultimate waste of time. Some of my friends had no such restraints.

One insisted that, if she was a winner, she would take out a contract with a car-valeting service so that her vehicle would be cleaned out and in regularly. Never again would she tackle that chore which she hated.

Another said she would have the whole house redecorated at once so, instead of going through the Forth Bridge syndrome, it would gleam from end to end all at the same time.

Katharine Whitehorn, the distinguished columnist, once wrote that her idea of being well off was being able to pay all the bills as they came in, instead of waiting for the monthly pay cheque.

And me? I would not know what to do with £500,000, would I? My lasting memory of that unreal afternoon in February is that I managed to spend half a million and more in less time than it takes to say "Scoop!".

I had bought a country house (with centrally heated kennels for a brace or two of English setters), booked a world cruise, invested in a whole new wardrobe, reserved seats on a regular basis at Covent Garden, presented my friends and relatives with a little token of my esteem ... well, there was not much change.

My friend was trying frantically to phone Vernons to make a claim. She made contact finally, only to be confused by a recorded volley of incomprehensible instructions.

She would not rest until someone else had confirmed the score — while I was installing myself mentally in my country house and looking forward to a world cruise.

A mutual friend, asked to check, brought us down to earth with a crash. Betty Rae (who used to own and run the Commercial Hotel at Inverurie with her late sister, Phyllis) gave us the explanation.

The total turned out to be a mere 17 and not 23 — the latter figure arrived at by erroneously adding the week's value of all 12 numbers instead of totalling only the eight best draws.

There was a short-lived sense of let-down, but nothing had changed. Except that I had learned to blow a mythical half million faster than anyone I know.

April 10, 1993

SECOND CHANCE

EXACTLY 20 years ago today, the first day of the rest of my life began. There I was, lying in a cubicle in the intensive-care unit of a Glasgow hospital, surrounded by a battery of monitor screens and flashing lights which reminded me of the cockpit of a Jumbo jet.

Silent figures, masked and gowned, moved noiselessly about the beds, whose occupants, from my prostrate position, I could hear — but I could not see. Feeling sore and drowsy, but enormously thankful and relieved, I lay, taking stock of my surroundings, listening to the music piped softly to the ward.

The first melody I heard, after a painful awakening, was a popular number of the day, sung by Cat Stevens to a familiar carol tune: Morning Has Broken.

I smiled secretly at the coincidence. For me, it was true in more ways than one. For me, morning truly had broken; the first of the rest of my life.

Not much do I remember about the previous day, except for the ecstatic effect of a pre-med drug they gave me before wheeling me rapturously to the table. It smoothed my path from ward to theatre where, for hours — while I hovered in that void somewhere beneath the conscious — surgeons struggled in an operation to try to arrest the progress of a rare neuromuscular disorder.

It is known as MG, short for myasthenia gravis, but the prognosis these days is mercifully better than it was then. Now, cures, or near-cures, are far from unknown. Then, they were rare, indeed.

It is a miserable and debilitating condition involving some of the body's most important muscles. Its symptoms include drooping eyelids, excessive fatigue, weakness of the limbs and difficulty in swallowing and breathing.

Because it is so rare, failure to diagnose 20 years ago was common, and most fatalities in those days, apparently, were due to that. My particular saga began in the summer of 1970.

72

An imminent general election meant that I had been even busier than usual, interviewing candidates in several constituencies.

I shrugged off persistent fatigue as natural until one weekend, while walking my dogs, I had an attack of breathlessness, so bad that I had to lie down in the heather to recover. I knew then that something was far wrong.

The family doctor, however, diagnosed flu and, after a few days' rest, I was back on the campaign trail. Then, one day, I was talking over the phone when my words began tumbling out in an incomprehensible jumble.

I knew what I wanted to say, but I could not make the right sounds. My speech let me down. Before I knew it, I was ensconced in a side ward in Aberdeen Royal Infirmary for tests. What did I have? A brain tumour? No, that was eliminated. Multiple sclerosis? That and other possibilities were ruled out. One week later, there was still no positive diagnosis.

I spent the time reading avidly in the peace and privacy of my little room and watching television — especially the political programmes — on my portable set in the corner. Came the eve of the poll and the doctors allowed me to watch as the results came in all through the night.

That turned out to be providential. Next morning, not surprisingly, I was tired out and failed every test of strength in the book. Later that day, my illness was diagnosed at last. For more than 18 months, increasing doses of prescribed drugs appeared neither to be controlling the symptoms nor the progress of the disease. I was referred to Professor J. Simpson in Glasgow (now retired) who, with a team as experienced in my illness as any anywhere, "strongly advised" surgery and was unable to predict what would happen without it. I had no choice.

Heavy shadows lay across my future. As I was driven to Glasgow two weeks ahead of my ordeal, I was aware that I could be looking at well-loved and familiar scenes for the last time.

In that fortnight, in the run-up to Deember 13, 1971, I came to know and love the warm-hearted Glasgow folk. Nurses cheered the day with their homely banter. Hard-working cleaners, in the early hours, never complained. I remember the elderly Glasgow woman at the city's Central Station who, with her brolly, fended off a pathetic drunk who accosted my sister, Norma, as she waited for the north train.

Gradually, I was accepted by my fellow-patients, many of whose lives had been very different from mine. Brave and stoic women they were, who simply accepted unquestioningly whatever hand fate dealt them. To each other, we confided our secret hopes and fears and drew mutual comfort in our world within a world.

Growing daily in strength after surgery, I went one evening to a carol service in another ward. Patients in wheelchairs, slippered and dressing-gowned, encircled those in bed as we sang the much-loved carols so redolent of childhood and happier days.

Suddenly, I felt sick for my cold, northern city; for my family and the familiar things of home.

Unlike me, not all of us made it home for Christmas. Sadly, one or two did not make it at all. I thought of them all fondly on Christmas Day 20 years ago as I savoured the most meaningful Yuletide ever. I think of them still, brief fellow-travellers, united in our different sufferings.

I do not believe any one emerges from an experience like that the same as before. For one thing, priorities are rearranged for ever in a world dominated by selfishness and greed.

And the gifts I was given at Christmas, 1971, are with me still — good health and a second chance.

What could be more precious?

December 14, 1991

Going for Gold

IF I knew enough about the psychology of selling, I suppose I could be luxuriating at this very moment in my very own villa in fair Provence or, for that matter, enjoying a sybaritic existence anywhere in the world. Instead, here I am, a poor scribe, spinning sentences for a living in dear old Aberdeen.

The truth is I know very little about selling and its techniques. Which is a pity. Not because I'd want to make a mint (and the top men certainly play for high stakes), but more as a matter of self-defence. I believe they do teach children in the schools these days something akin to consumer resistance, but that didn't happen in my day.

There is, though, one technique which I identified long ago and against which I am particularly on guard. They might have another name for it in the selling game. I call it ego massage.

You know the kind of thing. You tend to find it among your junk mail in the morning and the only difference is that it tells you: "You have been specially selected to go forward" or "Your name has been chosen for…"

Why me? It makes you feel just a mite important, doesn't it, first thing, among all the bills and reminders to pay and the daily pile of unsolicited rubbish which drops relentlessly through your letterbox?

It's no wonder, with such a blatant waste of paper, that each and every one of us is said to get through two trees shamelessly every year. But to get back to the message, the fact is that these examples are rather crude and old-hat, and it's a long time since I've become inured to that sort of selling.

And yet…

I reckon the company who offered me (as one of their specially chosen, greatly cherished VIP clients) their gold credit card the other day are lucky. Lucky that I declined their generous offer.

What would I want with one of these, I asked myself over

breakfast. They're for the yuppies of this world, really; for those who must make an impression; who need to broadcast their Gold credit rating.

But what about the practicalities? Look, you can have an advance of about £20,000 — and no questions asked — a small voice within persisted.

What would I do with £20,000, I countered. When am I going to need that sort of money in a hurry? I considered the matter over the cornflakes.

It's not such a lot these days. The small voice was persuasive. It wouldn't buy your permanent place in the sun, or a luxury yacht, or an original Monet, or any of the trappings of the wealthy, if that's what turns you on.

But it would finance a sudden rush of blood to the head or an expensive attack of midsummer madness. Which is precisely why I would be better without it. I turned it down in the end because I do not trust myself.

Besides, I have enough plastic already without any more — storecards, Access card, cheque cards, cashcards.

The only time, in fact, I've had to use my cashcard in an emergency, it disappeared down the tube, chewed up by the dispensing machine. Fortunately, the banks were open and all I had to do was cash a cheque. Otherwise, I would have had the embarrassment of trying to settle a taxi fare by cheque and paying for a round of drinks the same way.

More than once I have found myself staring blankly at the dispensing machine, having forgotten my personal number. Naturally, I have it written down, but it's in my diary and, when I swop handbags, I can forget the vital book and leave it behind.

My cashcard, though, is one piece of plastic I'd rather not be without. I have vivid memories of the days before they were invented, panicking in bank queues at the last minute, desperate to catch a train or plane.

Running out of "the readies" can lead to tricky situations and I take my hat off to one of my friends, a very cautious person, for her quick thinking. For much the same reasons as I rejected a Gold Card, she said "No" to a cashcard. The day came, as we suspected it would, when she ran out of money. I cannot

Never a more reluctant flowergirl than I. My aunt, Annie S. Murray, married Donald Thomson, Mains of Annochie, Auchnagatt, at Old Deer in 1940. See P63.

A welcoming kiss from former rector W.D. Kennedy when I revisited Fraserburgh Academy in 1969.

Blenda Briggs, of Alford, with two of her prize-winning Bennachie herd, Cameo, the kid, and Camilla.
See P80.

remember if the banks were closed or not but, in any case, she was nowhere near one.

Rushing into a big store, she bought a garment never intended to fit and paid for it by cheque. Soon afterwards, she returned it and was given a cash refund.

The real plus of the credit card, of course, is not so much that you can avoid carrying cash but that it allows you time to pay while your own funds languish in the bank attracting interest.

They are used for other reasons, too. A male friend, well known in his own community, charged his wife's anniversary present to his Access account because he didn't want the local bank staff to know how much her diamond brooch had cost.

But they have their disadvantages. A few days before Christmas, one of my colleagues found herself at a supermarket checkout with a couple of laden baskets and a long, impatient queue of shoppers behind her. She proffered her card but, without her knowing it, it was faulty.

The assistant held the card aloft and noisily summoned a supervisor. Embarrassed by the fuss and sensing 100 eyes upon her, my colleague blushed to the roots of her hair. It was not difficult to guess what the bystanders were thinking.

Ah, well. Now that I have rejected the Gold Card, I must remain in the ranks of the ordinary — a poor scribe spinning sentences for a living in dear old Aberdeen — and I would not swap that for anything.

July 1, 1989

BLENDA'S IDEA

IT WAS my cousin Blenda's idea. She is, in fact, my cousin thrice-removed, a relationship which some might consider quite remote — but I do not. A cousin is a cousin no matter what, sharing the same blood, however diluted; the same ancestry, for good or ill.

Blenda and I have in common, on our fathers' sides, great-grandparents who are really the nub of the story. Perhaps that should read "had" in common, for they are both long gone, sleeping together in the secluded kirkyard by the ruins of the mediaeval church of St Mary of Auchindoir, Aberdeenshire.

Bliss, it must be, to rest there, with the bones of their ancestors, for all eternity. For many generations lie still in that hallowed place at a wooded gorge with the Burn of Craig singing below.

But I digress. It was Blenda's idea, and a very good one it turned out to be.

"Why don't we all take a picnic and meet at the Aul Hoose at the Cabrach?" she suggested.

So it was that we foregathered in the heather on one of the few sunny Sundays in this dismal summer, at the wee place where our forefathers eked out an existence of sorts in what was little more than a peat bog.

Here, my great-grandparents reared 12 of a family, including my paternal grandfather — in which flock there might have been one black sheep at least. But not one, in their various lives, did ought to dishonour the family name. In fact, one or two did quite the opposite.

I stood in what was once the doorway, looking out over an expanse of moor stretching away to the foot of The Buck, the 2,368ft. landmark which dominates that bleak and barren landscape. The entire plateau of the Cabrach — the name derives from the Gaelic *caber,* meaning a tree — lies more than 1,000ft. above sea level.

Legend has it that the Cabrach was once a royal forest

belonging to Alexander III, but it was burned down on the orders of his queen.

It is said that Alexander, after a victory over Haco, King of Norway, visited the forest instead of going home to his queen, who was so enraged at this that she ordered the burning of the forest. This, the story goes, is why the Cabrach is almost treeless to this day.

It might seem improbable today, but this once-remote countryside was home to about 970 souls in 1831, before depopulation began, and in 1950 there were only 60 inhabited houses left, while the population totalled just 228.

Beyond the burn is the wee farm of Silverford, its cottage crumbling, from which a Gordon lad wooed and won a Murray lass, linking two names which ring proudly through Scotland's story and, what is more, bucking the trend of history.

Those two great clans could barely thole the sight of each other, and one instance of a dastardly deed is enshrined for ever in the old ballad. The Gordon Chieftain, in the reign of the tragic Queen of Scots, murdered the Bonnie Earl:

> *Oh, wae be tae ye, Huntly*
> *And wharfore did ye sae*
> *I bade ye bring him wi ye*
> *But forbad ye him to slay.*
> *He was a braw callant*
> *And he rid at the ring*
> *And the Bonnie Earl o' Moray*
> *He micht hae been a king.*

Blenda Briggs is a direct descendant of that Gordon-Murray marriage. Now, their grand-daughter is exploring the ruins, wondering what life was like for that large and happy brood, recounting anecdotes handed down from father to son. Last thing of a winter's night, they said, the old folk would take in a snow-shovel, ready to dig themselves out in the morning.

In those days, the snow lay deeper and longer on those high moors than anywhere else but, says the writer in the Statistical Account for 1791, "this was no inconvenience" because of the inexhaustible supply of peat on their doorsteps.

The crofters then tilled their land with a plough drawn by six, eight or 10 oxen. They grew barley, oats, potatoes, cabbages, and reared sheep and cattle. Their housework over, the womenfolk spun linen yarn and made coarse clothes for the family.

There was a lot of intermarriage. Most children went to school only in winter when they could be spared from herding the cattle. Even so, according to the writer, there was a high literacy rate, most being able to read and write.

"Nevertheless ... the tenants are in good circumstances enough for their rank," he reports, "and are thriving. They are mainly healthy and the most common disease from which they die is old age."

There, at the old road-end, my great-grandmother, in 1916, spotted the minister making his way to the house and her heart filled with dread for a son serving in France. Having broken the news, the good man tried to console the anguished mother.

"But, mistress," he soothed, "you've 11 more of a family."

"Aye," she retorted bitterly, "but I can spare not one."

No more with his siblings would he tramp the miles he once walked to school at Craig — late for the morning bell when, as the eldest boy at home, his chore was to carry water from the well.

In summer, his mother would take the fire to the water for the weekly washing, kindle it by the Craig Burn and boil the water on the spot. In winter, his father would fire a shot into the air when, in the dark, with snow filling the dykes, the home-coming children would take their direction from the report.

A crofter's wife, speaking at a meeting in 1936, said she remembered a market for cattle and horses. There were also lots of stands, and it was known as Mary Fair.

The drink supplied on that day was called "fechtin fusky", for the event seldom passed without some argument, which often ended in blows.

Long did we linger in the land of our fathers, but it was time to leave them resting at Auchindoir. What if they had been looking down from their celestial home? What would they have made of our little pilgrimage?

Roots worth having do not die with the days, but are nurtured by the years. Of that, I am quite sure.

FREE SPIRITS

TESSA and Tansy will be well and truly tubbed tonight, shampooed and set, primped and preened, for I want them to look their best tomorrow. I cannot think of much that Tansy enjoys more than a good grooming session. She stands in the shower, lifting her lovely face to the spray, half-closing her eyes as the water cascades over her, enjoying the fresh, clean feel of it.

Then, sybarite that she is, she proceeds to doze off under the warm air of the drier as she is blown and brushed until she gleams. I know that tomorrow she will be looking great, strolling on the Sabbath with her confident "look at me" air which she inherited from her ancestors.

Tansy, the stunning uptown girl, is almost Tessa's opposite. Tess is not at all partial to all the prettifying; tolerating the shower grudgingly, impatient with the blowing and drying routine, fed up with fuss. Dear, self-effacing, gentle Tess is a stay-at-home, happier by the fire than in the car; infinitely more content in everyday gear than dressed up for an outing.

Those who know about such things say that she does not have Tansy's classical good looks, but beauty is in the eye of the beholder — and I am the beholder.

Tonight, though, Tess must succumb; tomorrow, they are going to church.

What is so special about that, you might say. Nothing. Except that it is a special event, since they are not regular churchgoers, by any means. They go only once a year, and that by invitation.

They are not like you and me. They are of the animal kingdom. Tessa and Tansy are my much-loved dogs, my English setters, and tomorrow, at Craigiebuckler Church in Aberdeen, they will be in the congregation at a special animal-blessing service, organised by Aberdeen Association for the Prevention of Cruelty to Animals as a climax to National Pet Week.

There, in the open air, they will join a host of furred and feathered friends. Horses and hamsters, goats and guinea-pigs, cats and canaries. All are welcome, with owners old and young.

Especially the young. At animal-blessing services, now so popular throughout the country, a heartening feature is the attendance of the children, who are sometimes the main participants. They come bearing an assortment of creatures, great, but mainly small; in boxes, in baskets and on leads. It is one way of teaching them to value all life on earth.

In recent years, however, attendances at the blessing service in Aberdeen, sadly, have been disappointing, and it is hoped for a better response tomorrow. Perhaps numbers are affected by the weather, perhaps not. If the weather is not good, tomorrow's congregation will move indoors, to the church hall.

The church will not be used because the pews are thought to be too narrow to accommodate some of the animals. No matter, every creature present will be blessed by the Reverend James Thompson, formerly Episcopal priest of St Clement's in Aberdeen and now at Buckie.

He is one of Scotland's champions of animals and their rights; a man who — as vegetarian, anti-vivisectionist and outspoken opponent of factory farming — practises what he preaches. I do not necessarily agree with everything he advocates, but I admire enormously his courage in defending his convictions. He has been persecuted in defence of animals, once putting his job at risk and having to change denomination.

"The more they call me a nutter and a crank, the more I know I am succeeding," the mild-mannered clergyman once told me. "I know that God's concern and compassion envelop the whole of creation and not just one species within it," he said.

It has been his experience, as a pioneer of animal-blessing services, that there is no more commotion at one of those than there is at an average christening.

"The wolf also shall dwell with the lamb, and the leopard shall lie down with the kid and the calf and the young lion and the fatling together."

Animals in their own small groups can, of course, be quite tolerant of other species. We all know homes where dogs and cats live happily together — even if the dog then chases every other cat in the neighbourhood.

My excellent vet, David Wilson, quotes one household where there are rabbits and cats loose in the same house and another where a ferret sleeps with dogs and cats. Cats, however, are known for their independence, and those which curl up with goats and other animals are probably only opportunists — there for warmth, rather than out of friendship.

In some relationships, though, there is definitely more than tolerance. Horses are very sociable and willing to be friendly with anything. They hate being stuck on their own, and prefer another horse for company. If not, almost anything else will do.

One of the stories in, I think, All Creatures Great and Small, was about a horse which was diagnosed as having depression after its friend, a ram, was removed from the field. Its spirits lifted when the ram returned.

Friendships between species are sometimes a sort of maternal bonding where, for example, a newly hatched duckling will latch on to the first moving object it sees as it enters the world. I know someone who had a duck which followed her everywhere, even to work.

In the end, the strongest friendships are probably between the same species. Tansy and Duke (not their posh names, by the way) struck up an instant rapport when they appeared in the same showring. They played together and rolled over and over when they met as puppies, and their love was lasting and touching. Duke's owner, Mrs Kath Balharrie, of Culloden, knew when I had arrived in the hall — before she saw me — because Duke suddenly became so excited as he sensed Tansy's arrival.

Tansy missed more than a year of attendance at shows and did not see Duke during that time. Finally, she returned to the showring at Bo'ness where there were hundreds of setters that day. Between classes, Tansy was reintroduced to Duke.

Recognition took only a moment and the reunion was something to behold. They rubbed faces, licked each other and rolled over and over in joy. I hope Duke is not there tomorrow.

Finally, I have heard it said that you can tell how civilised a society is by how it treats its old and its sick. I have something to add to that: I would say you can tell by how it treats its old, its sick — and all the animals entrusted to its care.

STORM WARNING

HERE I was feeling very smug, investing one day last week in a thermal vest as my personal guarantee of a good winter. Now, there was a time, I do confess, when a "good" winter meant one with lots of snow, when much fun was to be had on sparkling moonlit nights skating on the lake in the grounds of crumbling Strichen House or tobogganing at speed down the steep brae from the local hospital.

Once, the story goes, a lad was sledging down so fast that he could not stop and he and his sledge went clean under an oncoming ambulance to emerge unscathed at the other end. Apocryphal or not, the big sixth-year boys talked about it in hushed tones as if the feat were something to be emulated.

That is not the kind of winter I enjoy nowadays and, for the past year or two, I have been lucky. The winters have been good — and, by that, I mean relatively snow-free. This might be due, I have heard it said, to the greenhouse effect which is allegedly warming up our world. Maybe so, but I prefer to take my own precautions.

After that winter a few years ago when parts of the Northeast were without electricity for up to three weeks, I invested in a generator. It would at least keep the heating going and one ring of the cooker and maybe even the telly — and I would settle for that.

It wasn't so much heating up the baked beans on a picnic stove by candlelight that got to me. It was more the fact that an entire heating system was brought to a standstill because there was no electricity to operate the pump.

Not that I understand these things. In fact, I have thought about having a practice run at starting the generator, bearing in mind that it is a routine which would probably have to be done in the dark and which involves rather more than merely pressing a switch.

But, predictably, I haven't and, in any case, I'm sure I used its petrol for the lawnmower in the summer.

That machine, however, has been worth every penny, since there hasn't been even a hiccup in the electricity supply since the day it came home.

Much the same can be said about my Jeep with its amazing four-wheel-drive, a facility I have used in a serious way only once — on a blazing summer's day when I ditched it while turning on a narrow, moorland road.

But one good reason for the Jeep, as opposed to buying a conventional car, was my resolve that days of pushing vehicles out of snowdrifts or ditches or up slippery slopes were over.

So far, my Jeep has kept the storms away, but that is not the only reason why I don't regret having it. Which is another story.

As for winters, it seems as if they aren't anything as bad as they used to be. I remember when trains got stuck regularly in the snow on the Buchan line for hours or days before they were rescued.

Once, when supplies were depleted, my uncle, Donald Thomson, walked the distance from Auchnagatt to Maud in a whiteout to buy bread. That happened — if my memory is right — in a notorious storm in the early 1940s. In those days, I don't suppose there was anything unusual in an effort like that.

It doesn't seem so long ago, though, when we were totally dependent in the country on delivery vans. One butcher, I recall, used to leave what he guessed I would need at the cottage half a mile away and he would be paid next time round.

The deep freeze and front-wheel-drive cars have revolutionised winter living in the country. The slightest hill became a slippery, insurmountable obstacle before the time of front-wheel drive.

Wattie Simpson, a jovial farmer with tractor and storm lantern, was a welcome sight at the bottom of our brae when we were at the end of a tiring day and battling to get home in the dark. He used to wait patiently in the cold, about 20 years ago, to make sure his neighbour commuters got home.

As one after another tried, and failed, to get up the hill, Wattie, who used to farm Little Banchory at Banchory-Devenick, would tow us up with his tractor and with cheery wave, set us on the last lap. That sort of warm community spirit seems, like so many things, to have vanished.

But it wasn't all a struggle; there was some fun, too. One snowbound Hogmanay, friends arrived to first-foot on skis at a time when they were virtually unknown in this country. I had seen skis before, but only on postcards. The first day of that New Year was spent trying to master the difficult art and, to this day, I have not.

Social life in the winter was very active; so hectic, in fact, that there came a time when one longed for a good reason to turn down an invitation. "I don't want to be snowed up" was one excuse I proffered for not going to a party. I stayed at home and had my comeuppance. I was snowed in for three whole days.

There was nothing I could do about a long-standing engagement I had agreed to fulfil at a big and very formal affair. Well, the wind rose, the snows fell and the lights went out. Ever tried to get ready, by the light of a candle propped up at the end of a bath?

Today, there is some snow about. In fact, I think I'll go now to check the Jeep and start the generator instead of sitting here in my thermal vest feeling very smug.

December 4, 1988

Auld Lang Syne

Rise up, aul wife, and shak yer feathers.
Dinna think that we are beggars;
We're only bairnies come ti play.
Rise up and gie's wir Hogmanay.

WHEN I was at primary school in the Buchan village of Stuartfield, my brother, sister and I hung up our stockings for Santa on Christmas Eve. But, among our classmates in those pre-war days, we were in the minority.

Not so long ago, Santa came to most children on New Year's Eve, when bands of excited youngsters in our village, as well as in many others, went from house to house, chanting a traditional rhyme like the one above as they sought their "Hogmanay".

Invariably, they were given something small, usually a sweetie, a ha'penny or maybe an apple or an orange. As children, we were less than enchanted at being forbidden to go on these harmless Hogmanay rounds. My parents, I suspect, thought it too much like begging.

In the early hours of New Year's Day, I remember being awakened by the sounds of revelry as first-footers moved from house to house, celebrating and visiting, until well into the first day of the year. The whole village seemed to be on the move.

Hogmanay is no longer what it was; drink-driving laws almost put an end to first-footing, especially in country areas. I remember well when every chair in the house was taken long before midnight and there was standing room only for early first-footers. Then, fortifying ourselves with little gifts as "handsel", we would join the others and move off in groups on a round of our neighbours.

Traditionally, a first-footer arriving empty-handed was a sign of poverty and privation for the household in the year ahead and, to this day, what first-footers there are generally carry handsel. It can be anything from a bottle of whisky to a piece of Black Bun or an orange. They are given something to eat and drink before continuing on their rounds or staying to join in the celebrations.

For many years, my brother, Kenny, was our first foot, knocking loudly as soon as the midnight bells had ceased, bearing in his hands some peat or a lump or two of coal. For generations, fuel was a popular "handsel"; a practice rooted in an old belief that fire destroys evil. Even now, people still take in a peat, a lump of coal or a small log and place it on the fire.

In the old days, apparently, the fire was kept burning until the New Year was in. To allow it to go out presaged, it was thought, a death in the house before the year's end.

All sorts of rituals were followed in days gone by to dispel evil spirits, and to make sure that the coming year was one of good fortune. One priority was that the house should be cleaned out meticulously, for it was thought that, in this way, the ill luck of the past 12 months was driven out.

All the housework, every last chore, had to be complete by the last day of the old year. If anything was left undone, superstition had it that matrimonial aspiration would not materialise.

The Christmas clean is nothing new to me; I have clear memories of it. In fact, I know that many people carry it out still. Even now, our chimney-sweep is so booked up at Christmas that, unless your appointment is made early, he will be too busy to come until the new year.

Hogmanay was steeped in superstition and I am not familiar with many of the old customs and rites which have almost vanished.

For example, I did not know that once, after the Christmas cleaning, a Bible was placed above the door in the last hours of the year. This was to stop evil powers re-entering the house. The cat was kept inside so that, if any unlucky first-foot came in, the evil could be shed by throwing out the cat!

By 8pm on Hogmanay, some of our predecessors were seemingly scanning the sky carefully. Importance was attached to the last night of the year in forecasting the weather and the fertility of the land in the 12 months ahead.

If, for example, the largest cloud in the sky away to the north was black and had a soft and not a frosty appearance, the year would be one of plenty for man and beast.

If, on the other hand, the cloud lay to the east, the year would be fairly good; to the south, there would be plenty straw but little grain. If the sky was cloudless, the year would be bad.

As the hands of the clock were almost on the midnight hour, the head of the house rose, went to the door and opened it wide. He held the door like that until the last stroke of the hour died away. Then, finally, shutting the door, he rejoined the family, having let the old year out and the new year in.

In some parts of the Highlands, the man of the house used to go to the back door in the closing minutes of the year and fire a shot into the sky. He would then rush round to the front door to greet the new year with a skirl of his bagpipes.

A dark, handsome man is still considered in the North-east the "luckiest" of all first-foots. In these parts, fair men were taboo; a prejudice which, some say, dates to the Norse invasions.

Unlucky first-foots are anyone carrying a knife, or anyone wearing black. If an unwelcome first-foot appeared, there were ways of avoiding ill-luck — throwing salt on the fire before he came in; having the first word with him; making a sign of the cross, or by burning something like a wisp of straw.

Two fire ceremonies have survived in the North-east: Burning the Clavie at Burghead, and Swinging the Fireballs at Stonehaven. On the afternoon of January 11 at Burghead, young men prepare a tar barrel, or Clavie. Towards sunset, it is set alight and the Clavie-bearer goes round the village with his blazing burden. Then, when the procession ends outside the village, the Clavie is placed on a stone pillar, more fuel is piled in it and it burns for another half-hour.

At Stonehaven, the original idea of Swinging the Fireballs on New Year's Eve was to drive away evil spirits from the local fishing boats. Nowadays, New Year is mainly the time for family gatherings and reunions, when people travel many hundreds of miles to be together in Scotland — for the sake of Auld Lang Syne.

A LITTLE MITE

I T MEASURES less than an inch from tip to tail and that is
when it has been magnified 85 times. It looks rather like a
crab, but infinitely smaller — so minute, in fact, that it is
invisible to the naked eye. For something so small, it has
caused me a disproportionate amount of pain and trouble. I am
talking about the house dust-mite, a fashionable topic these
days

These are the culprits which spawn the potent allergens, the
cause of asthma in humans and skin trouble in dogs and I have
declared war on them.

Like most women, I seem to have spent a fair proportion of
my adult life cleaning the house, sometimes with help,
sometimes without. It is not, I must say, a job I enjoy, except
that I loathe untidiness even more, finding it irksome and
unsettling until all is done and in its proper place.

I suppose it is the monotony of it which I dislike; the repeti-
tiveness of it; the same old thing, vacuuming, dusting,
polishing, day after day. But still there is dust — and, yes, I
have dust-mites and so, apparently, has everyone else.

"It does not mean that your house is not clean," a specialist
soothed as he noted my look of astonishment.

The truth is that I have managed to live with them peacefully
all these years without any problems. They did not bother me
unduly, although I must have realised they were there. Then,
early this summer, my four-year-old English setter began to
itch.

At first, I thought she had picked up something nasty in the
woods, but regular lice-killing baths made not the slightest difference and the house reeked constantly of hospitals.

The vet at first suspected an allergy caused, most likely, by
brushing against something — in the forest, on the beach or in
the garden? Angry pink patches began to appear on her legs,
her ears, her underbelly. She scratched constantly.

Would I like a specialist opinion in the full understanding
that even a doggy dermatologist might not be able to pinpoint

the allergens? I had visions of regular trips with Tansy in tow to the Royal Dick in Edinburgh or the animal hospital in Glasgow.

That, as it happened, was not necessary. We found just such an excellent chap in ordinary practice in, of all places, the Buchan countryside. He understood my anxiety. He was sympathetic. His grasp of his subject was impressive. Something had to be done, and quickly. By this time, the quality of her life was waning. I would hear her scratching, scratching endlessly, in the night, when even sleep was disturbed by the constant itch. There was no respite.

I would get up and bathe her burning skin with cold, damp cloths, but the relief was short-lived. In the silence, she would look at me with soulful eyes. "Help me, please," they seemed to say. Then began the process of elimination. For three weeks, a bland diet of nothing but boiled rice and lamb with water, no milk. Our hopes were raised and dashed as she appeared to improve only to relapse. In the end, food was eliminated as a cause.

The next step was a series of tests which, we prayed, would produce a positive diagnosis. Her silky flank was shaved and the tests were conducted under sedation. They proved conclusively that she was allergic to the house dust-mite and to human dandrum, which is just a fancy word for dead skin.

It was likely to be a life-long problem, the expert explained, but there were, thankfully, several ways of treating her and improving the quality of her life. I felt as if he had handed me a million pounds.

She was put on a course of steroids immediately, while a vaccine, tailored to her requirements, was ordered from Holland. Then we could consider keeping her outside — never a realistic solution; she is a pet, used to living indoors, and who would want to end up in a kennel on a cold, stormy night? I suspect that it would not be Tansy.

The steroids worked almost at once and all her verve and love of life returned. It is sheer delight to watch her romp with Tessa, her life-long friend, in the woods. Now the steroids have been dropped and she is having regular injections of the vaccine, which we trust will work.

And what about the house dust-mites? Do you think I would let them off scot-free after all this trouble? The heavy artillery arrived the other day in the shape of a big vacuum-cleaner, designed especially to combat house dust-mites. My old one owed me nothing, anyway.

The allergens from mites, apparently, are so small that ordinary vacuum-cleaners cannot retain them and reportedly blow out as much as 40% of them into the atmosphere, aggravating the condition.

I have no way of knowing if any improvement is due to the vaccine, or the machine or both.

Now I will go to my vacuum-cleaning with a will. I can think of no better incentive for doing the housework than managing to massacre millions of the dreaded house dust-mites.

October 12, 1991

● *Tansy has responded well to her treatment and enjoys a very good quality of life, despite her allergies*

RED POPPIES

THIS week, I bought a couple of red Flanders poppies, which are lying here in front of me as I write. I bought them in memory of two unknown soldiers — they were, at least, unknown to me.

If the truth be told, I did not need the poppies to remind me of them. Like thousands of others this month, I got them to support an excellent cause. But, every now and then, as I caught sight of them lying here, they set me thinking ...

And the outcome is that they inspired me to plan a pilgrimage which, if I do not make, I will regret for the rest of my life.

In World War II, our family was extremely fortunate. Despite having someone in all three of the Armed Services, every one came home, maybe with a physical wound and emotional scarring, but perfectly able to pick up the threads of their lives again.

Of course, that is not to say that I cannot empathise deeply with those thousands who did lose someone and whose thoughts turn, particularly at this time of the year, to their memory.

I believe strongly that Remembrance Sunday should not be allowed to lapse. Remembrance rituals do not, in my view, glorify war; rather do they highlight the horror and the suffering and the pity of it. That might be particularly relevant this year in view of the situation in the Gulf.

Tonight, with countless thousands, I will watch the Festival of Remembrance from the Albert Hall, proud to see the clean-cut young men in their polished uniforms; sad to count the poppies as they fall on the frail shoulders of the little band of Chelsea pensioners.

And, tomorrow, I will not be alone in praying, during the religious ceremonies, for a diplomatic solution to the crisis in the Middle East.

Through it all, however, two individuals will be uppermost in my own memory; two uncles I did not have the privilege to know who died in France in the holocaust which was World War I.

They were, more accurately, my great-uncles and the fact that I did not know them does not seem to change a thing. Those who loved them — almost all gone now — never did forget them. Their names cropped up naturally in conversation as if they had not gone far away; as if they had not really gone at all.

As children, we were taught to honour them and to value their sacrifice. But to us, ignorant of the minutiae of their lives, they were inevitably shadowy figures, family members who were always there in the background. For that reason, they assumed a mystique, the status of heroes.

So what were they really like, those two of my own flesh and blood who fell in France so long ago? How did they die? In which battles? Where are their graves? Do they have graves? I was seized by an urgent need to know.

John C. Robertson, from Speyside (my grandmother's brother), served in the Cameron Highlanders, and Alex Murray, from Banffshire (my grandfather's brother), had emigrated to New Zealand and joined the Army there — but which Army, British or New Zealand? It was not much to go on.

Then there began a detective hunt which took me all the way from the Cameron Barracks in Inverness, through the Army Records Office and the Medal Records Office to the Commonwealth Graves Commission.

On the face of it, it seemed a simple matter to get the necessary information from the Army Records Office. But it was not.

For one thing, the personal records held by them are confidential and are not released without the written consent of the next-of-kin and payment of a £15 fee.

For another, they deal with 3000 queries a month and, in any case, only 40% of World War I records survive, the others having been destroyed in a blitz in World War II.

It is incredible to think that I am now John's next-of-kin: all his nearer relatives long gone.

Within half an hour, Lt-Col. Angus Fairrie, the knowledgeable regimental secretary of the Queen's Own Highlanders — through them, of course, the Camerons live on — had most of the information I wanted.

Pte. John Robertson, of the 7th Bn., the Cameron Highlanders, fell in the Battle of Loos on September 25, 1915. That, said Col. Fairrie, was one of the saddest days in British history.

The Cameron Highlanders went into action 629 strong and, in the end, only 81 remained to fight next day, their comrades having been wounded or taken prisoner or killed.

Descriptions of the battle make gruesome reading. The early British offensive was as disastrous as it was indecisive.

John never returned to the young wife he married on his last leave and who had only a few days with her new husband.

No cross marks the spot where he lies — only an inscription to his memory on the war memorial at Loos.

Almost exactly a year later, in September, 1916, Alex was killed in the Battle of the Somme. In that dread September, 101,313 British soldiers lost their lives at the Somme alone.

From the date and history books, I deduce that he must have taken part in the third British attack of the battle of Flers.

We know that Alex died bravely on the field of battle, but I can unearth nothing more until his rank and regiment — at least — are known. That will lead me soon to detailed local research.

It matters not that there might be no known graves to visit. I will go whatever, bearing some purple heather so that these corners of that foreign field will be forever Scotland. So that, from their places in the sunset, they will know somehow that they are not forgotten.

November 10, 1990

ROYAL REVELS

THE last time a Royal invitation arrived, I was forced through illness to turn it down. It was to attend Her Majesty's garden party at the Palace of Holyroodhouse in the early Seventies. Before you think that I am getting a little above myself, let me say at once that Royal invitations do not drop through my letterbox every day. In fact, until then, I had not received a single one.

You can imagine the disappointment I felt at having to decline. Indeed, I considered writing a postcript on my reply, saying: "Please ask me again another time." Of course, I did no such thing. It simply is not done.

At last, the day came and, if I remember rightly, the weather was kind. Feeling somewhat left out at home, I was dispirited, imagining the scene in Edinburgh as the well-dressed guests mingled on the lawns of Holyrood, awaiting the entrance of Her Majesty.

You do not, I think, have to be a royalist to react to the presence of royalty. The most dedicated republican might feel the rising excitement as the moment approaches, the butterflies in the tummy, if there is the slightest chance of being presented. There is the familiar lump in the throat, for most of us, a sense of patriotism and pride and wonderment that the slight figure of the monarch symbolises so much.

I have not, I may say, had the honour of being presented to her myself — although I have seen all her family, sometimes at very close quarters over the years — but I have had the pleasure of meeting the Queen Mother and the effervescent Princess Alexandra.

The Queen Mother came — in 1972, I think it was — to look over the new offices of Aberdeen Journals in the Mastrick area of Aberdeen. Yes, it's true what they say — she really does make you feel that you are the only person who matters all the time you are conversing.

I remember the celebrated complexion, the sheer blueness of

the eyes but, perhaps most of all, I remember how well she had done her homework. My name — as a newspaper executive of the day and not writing much for print — she could not be expected to know. But know it she did, as well as that of my respected colleague, the late Dr Cuthbert Graham. She had considerable knowledge, too, of what our jobs were and she talked to us about it easily and in an informed way.

Earlier, in the late Sixties, I had the honour to be presented to Princess Alexandra who, as patron of the Guide Dogs for the Blind Association, was attending a reception in Aberdeen's Beach Ballroom. At that time, through the newspaper, I was involved in mobilising the efforts of children and young people throughout the northern half of Scotland in raising money to train dogs for the blind.

Our aim was to make enough to supply all the trained dogs to clear the Scottish waiting list and, at the time of the reception, we seemed set fair to do just that (we did it in the end). The reception was not organised by the newspaper nor by anyone connected with it, so we had no clear idea of who was to be there and who was not. It was generally accepted, though, that the Princess's presence was a tacit acknowledgement of all the hard work put in by the youngsters.And so it turned out.

"Would you be good enough to introduce Her Royal Highness to some of your young fund-raisers?" the Princess's lady-in-waiting asked. So I guided the royal visitor towards this group and that and, to my increasing discomfiture, failed to find even one little party of children, even one small child, who had worked for our scheme.

Most of the pupils present, it transpired, came from fee-paying schools, few of which had lifted as much as a finger then to raise money for our scheme — a fact which, by the end of the day was patently obvious to an astonished Princess.

Now, what was I coming to? Yes, through my letterbox the other day dropped — you've guessed it — a royal invitation. It came from Alice, Duchess of Gloucester, president of Scotland's Gardens Scheme, to attend, in the presence of the Queen, a garden party at Holyroodhouse on July 2, to mark the diamond jubilee of the scheme.

This time, God willing, I will be there. I have long admired those owners of gardens in castle and in cottage — as well, naturally, as the gardeners themselves — who open their gardens to the public in aid of charity. In Scotland, 300 gardens open under the scheme annually, of which 19 are in Grampian, where the joint organisers are Mrs Wolrige Gordon, of Esslemont, and Mrs J.A. Dingwall-Fordyce, West Affleck, Maud, and the honorary secretary and treasurer is Miss C.T. Reid from Tarves.

I hope to meet them soon, together with others who work tirelessly for the scheme at the royal garden party. I am looking forward to that.

June 29, 1991

NIGHT RAIDER

I T WAS the week before Christmas and the house was very still. Nothing stirred as I sat up late writing last-minute cards and seasonal letters. Suddenly, on the ceiling above, there was a loud thump.

"Naughty girl!" I exclaimed out loud, assuming that Tess, my English setter, had rediscovered the delights of a duvet and, after enjoying a furtive nap, was jumping off the bed.

I went to check, ready to deliver a scolding. But, lo and behold, I found Tess and Tansy tucked up in their respective beds in the usual place by the radiator.

I froze with fear as the realisation came. I had a two-legged intruder or a four-legged one and neither was welcome. Sensing my fear, the dogs looked puzzled and nuzzled me with their soft heads, as if to say: "Don't worry. We'll look after you."

They would, too. I have little doubt about that. English setters are the gentlest of creatures, but they are big dogs and would not hesitate to retaliate in a threatening situation.

Obviously, they had heard nothing. Even now, they gave no sign of discomfiture or awareness — which, almost certainly, they would have done if there was a stranger in the house.

Suddenly, there it was again. Thump! On the ceiling above, this time followed by loud, noisy scurryings in the floorboards. The dogs cocked their heads, listened momentarily and lost interest.

I shut the door firmly behind me, leaving the cards and things untidied on the table, and hurried to the other end of the house where some embers still glowed on the living-room fire. Propped up by a large dog on either side, I settled on the sofa. Their nearness was soothing; their warmth comforting and soon they fell sound asleep. That was the last thing I could do.

I would not describe myself as the most courageous person in the world, although I am no coward, either. But seldom have the dark hours passed so slowly. Whenever a dog stirred or a rafter creaked, my heart missed a beat. But could I have been mistaken? Was it merely a mouse sheltering from the cold? No, the footfalls had been too heavy. They could have been wearing hob-nailed boots.

Friends have since told me that I have been very fortunate to have lived in the country for so many years without confronting a rat; without coming face to face with one, if you know what I mean. I have seen them, of course, picking one out occasionally in the beam of the headlights after dark.

I remember, too, watching them scurrying from the corn ricks as the farmworkers forked the sheaves into the jaws of a threshing mill. The men, I was told, wore nicky-tams to prevent the brutes running up their legs.

Was it not the lore surrounding them — the stories I had heard about their cunning, their filth, their disease-carrying capacity — which now invoked this terror? Without success, I tried to rationalise it but, for me, they remain the stuff of nightmares. Have we not heard — whether true or false — reports of their having bitten babies in their cots and, when cornered, attacking fully grown men? In the long reaches of that night, it all came back and, in the end, my intruder had assumed such proportions that I would rather have tackled a tiger.

I remembered a lorry-driver describing graphically how one night his headlamps picked up countless tiny lights in the dark. As he drew closer, he realised he had come across rats on the move, known as a rats' "flitting". They were everywhere, rushing across the road, jumping out from dykes and hedgerows, rushing endlessly into his path. It was, he said, one of the most frightening things he had ever experienced.

I recalled, too, the farmer's wife who told me how she was awakened by a rhythmic thump-thump in a downstairs corridor which passed the milkhouse where she stored her home-made cheese and eggs. She vowed that, rising, she saw several rats lying on their backs in a rodent chain, passing eggs hand-over-hand, one to the other.

Some time before the dawn, sleep had at last overtaken me, but not before I had formulated a plan of action. Next day, in response to an urgent summons, Ronald MacKintosh — who runs his own pest-control business in Aberdeen — arrived

With my brother, Kenny, and sister, Norma, at his 21st birthday party at the Saltoun Hotel in 1954. He was Fraserburgh FC's centre-forward at the time.

*Mrs Ella Christie (left), Miss Margaret Barron, both of New Deer,
and Mr Alistair Cruickshank, Fyvie, feeding the hens
at Hareshowe Croft, Aden Park. See P15.*

*Reunited half-sisters Mrs Sybil McIntosh, of Stonehaven (right),
and Mrs Babs Smith, Pitcaple. See P60.*

promptly. He searched the garden; he looked in the garage. There, he found traces which confirmed the worst suspicion. The good news was, he thought, only one, a straggler, which he hoped to eradicate with poison.

He laid the poison in strategic places and promised to return next day. It had not occurred to me that it would take time to exterminate. Somehow, I had thought it would be all over in a matter of minutes instead of an estimated four or even five days.

It was clearly an ordeal I could not endure. Sheepishly, I described the emergency to my sister, Norma, and her husband, Simon, on the phone. "You must come and stay," they insisted.

Once there, I was told by them, sympathetically, that they would not have been able to cope, either, and that, one day, I might have to return the favour. That made me feel better as I kept in touch by phone with events at home.

For two nights, I stayed away while Mr MacKintosh dealt with the problem. On the third day, he was fairly sure that the coast was clear. The poison that he had laid had been taken and he had also found the entry — a hole in the foundations made by scraping away loose cement to gain access to the old, rubble walls.

Since then, I have not had time to contact the environmental-health people to inquire if they have a pest-control officer — and if not, why not.

January 4, 1992

Swallow Tales

O N A DAY of baking heat in this amazing summer, four little ones first saw the light of day in a shady corner deep in the recesses of my garage. Their parents arrived on June 5, quite unexpectedly and literally out of the blue. I know it was June 5 because I noted it in my diary at the time.

Quite an auspicious day it was because they had not visited for years and we had missed them. Often, agonising over their absence, we would speculate as to why we had been ... so unceremoniously ... dumped.

They must have thought us inhospitable, we concluded, arriving all that way from Africa to find the door shut tight in their faces. Inhospitable, to say the least. The real reason was a growing security-consciousness.

Time was, here in the country, where everyone knows everyone else, that it wasn't considered essential to lock one's doors at night.

But those days are long gone and locking up at night, including the garage, is merely a matter of routine.

This year, on the day they arrived, the garage door was open. They came out of a clear, blue sky, swooping and whirling, skimming and diving, clearly looking for a place to stay. We knew they would settle only if they could come and go as they pleased.

"Leave your car locked outside and the garage door open," advised a friend who, in any case, does not believe in garages. His theory, incidentally, is that a car outside dries off more quickly and therefore rusts less than if indoors.

In any case, that is what I did. One swallow, they say, does not make a summer, but now we have six. As day followed sun-filled day, life tended to centre on the garden where we watched the little parents swooping out and in, building their nest — an extraordinary feat if ever there was. The activity was frantic and they would rest only occasionally, perched side by side on the telephone wire like two posh waiters in their white tie and tails.

My English setters, normally fascinated by feathered frolics, were too hot to be bothered. They languished flat-out on the lawn, before wandering indoors to find a cool spot under an open window.

The heatwave continued and deck-chair days sped by. Increasingly, as they found it unbearable, the dogs were spending more and more time inside until they found their own novel, if disruptive, solution. If I were asked, I'd take a bet that Tansy was the instigator: Tansy, the confident; Tansy, the font of all mischief and mayhem. She simply turned night into day and Tess — dear, kind Tess — obliged.

More than once, on a midsummer midnight, I was amused by their canine capers in the twilight. It was cooler then and once, in the shadows, they cornered Mole. They were bewildered totally. Never had they seen such a creature and they stood around him, barking.

All day they had been fascinated by his tell-tale humps, burrowing furiously, scattering clouds of earth as they sensed his subterranean presence. Now Tess waited for Tansy to take the initiative — which she did, prodding the poor blind beast with her paw and leaping back swiftly before he could react. Mole had long since made his escape before their excitement subsided.

By the first week in July, there were umistakable sounds of new life in the nest. How many chicks, we wondered? Would they fly off and never return? Or would they come back next year?

By coincidence, a young man came pedalling by one evening on his bicycle, who could answer some, if not all, of our questions. He noticed the parent birds wheeling and swooping by the garage entrance.

"Do you mind if I look at your swallows?" Ian Rendall asked politely. Of course we didn't, especially when we learned that his hobby is "ringing" birds; attaching a tiny ring to one of their legs with an individual number and the address of the British Museum in London. This way, information can be gathered about the birds — where they have come from, how far they have travelled, and so on.

But ringing birds is not something just anyone can do. Ian is a member of the 25-strong Grampian Ringing Group, where he trained in all aspects of ringing to gain a permit.

It's quite a tricky business, apparently. Ringers use a pliers to attach the ring to the tiny legs. Obviously, they have to be extremely careful to avoid hurt and they must know, for instance, how to take the ring off the fragile limb if it goes on in the wrong way.

According to Ian, it is rare that a bird dies as a result of their activities, although sometimes they do suffer from shock, which is apparently one reason why some birdwatchers object to ringing.

Our four chicks are flying now, and sometimes, as they perch on the wire, I fancy I catch the glint of the metal rings in the sun. Already the mother bird is sitting on her second clutch of eggs and Ian will be back in two weeks to ring these, too, as well as their parents.

Today, with a pang, I saw some swallows flocking on the wires at the end of the road. Soon, too soon, they will be off on their long journey to Africa, resting their little bodies on the way on ships' masts or oilrigs or in oases in the baking desert.

Will we see them again? Will they return next year? In due course, we might be able to answer that, for Ian is determined to come back next summer to check.

Meanwhile, I cannot bear to watch them go; to see them set out on their formidable flight through the pathless air, when all I can do is hope and pray that all their landings will be happy ones.

August 5, 1989

AT THE GATE

BY THE time you read this, the year will be six days old and many a New Year resolution will already be broken. I am writing as the last hours of the old year die away and I must say that not a single resolution have I made. By the time you read this, too, the day will have come, a day I disliked as a child, when the tree is at last dismantled, the cards come down and the house is generally stripped of its festive trappings.

January 6 signalled the end of the Christmas celebrations and how bare and cheerless everything seemed without the colourful glitter. It was imperative, I seem to recall, to have the decorations down on Twelfth Night if bad luck was to be averted in the coming year.

A great deal of superstition attached to this, if I remember rightly, and one of my friends assures me that her mother would never put up the holly before December 24, never take it down before Twelfth Night and, when she did, she would never burn it.

The snag is, though, that nobody appears to be quite sure exactly when Twelfth Night is. It appears to be in how you interpret it and my dictionary legitimises both the evening of January 5 (as the eve of Twelfth Night) and the evening of January 6.

Today also marks the Christian festival of Epiphany which, since the fourth century, has traditionally ended the Christmas merrymaking. Indeed, in some countries, gifts are exchanged today as symbols of the presents the Wise Men gave to the infant Jesus. In fact, Epiphany — the word means manifestation — has come to be associated with the meeting of the three Wise Men and the baby Jesus.

There were, of course, many other pagan festivals and customs around this time which marked the turning of the year — Burning the Clavie and Up-Helly-Aa are two which survive.

Nowadays, I don't mind at all the decorations coming down.

Garish and dog-eared they seem by this time and, in any case, their demise heralds a welcome return to normality. As I grow older, I prefer, too, to see the shortest day behind me. Do you know, as you read this, that there is 15 minutes' more daylight today than there was on December 21? It is, somehow, a time of new beginnings ... and fresh hope.

Looking back at what I have written at the beginning of more successive years than I like to admit, the consistent theme has been the hope for an easing of East-West tensions, for world peace. Now, as we enter the 1990s, there are, perhaps for the first time, genuine reasons to hope for nothing less. To those of us who have lived under the shadow of The Bomb and with the threat of nuclear holocaust, that is indescribable.

Certainly, I have never been more conscious of living through history as I was in the closing weeks of 1989 as the momentous events in Eastern Europe unfolded. Never in my wildest dreams did I think I would live to see the crumbling of the Berlin Wall. Did any of us?

Was it only five years ago that Mikhail Gorbachev emerged to herald a new age of perestroika? He seems to have been around a lot longer than that, and one prayer must be that he survives all domestic difficulties for the sake of global stability. He must surely go down as one of the towering figures of the 20th century.

Nobody, until the decade approached its half-way stage, had heard of Aids or of the Greenhouse Effect — two phenomena with enormous implications for the future. If sanity prevails, Aids will revolutionise sexual behaviour so that not one innocent victim will be affected by the horrible scourge. But something tells me this is too much to ask.

The Greenhouse Effect might actually have the bonus of uniting the nations of the world in a concerted effort to save our planet; to conserve some of the creatures who share it with us and whose rights ought to be recognised more keenly.

Very remote now appear some of the events at the start of the 1980s. It was only in 1980 that the British flag was lowered in Britain's last African colony and Rhodesia became Zimbabwe. That seems like light years ago.

But some things don't change. In East Africa 10 years ago,

millions faced the world's worst famine because of drought, pestilence and local wars. The developed world rushed to their aid but, although there might not be much we can do about the natural element of global disasters, perhaps we could do something about the wars?

Nearer to home, the other insurmountable problem was the troubles in Northern Ireland, which have permeated the 1980s like a festering sore. Our resolve must be never to give in to terrorism wherever it is found.

And I said to the man who stood at the gate of the year: 'Give me a light that I may tread safely into the unknown.' And he replied: 'Go out into the darkness and put your hand into the hand of God. That shall be to you better than light and safer than a known way.'

January 6, 1990

AVOIRDUPOIS

THERE was a time, not many hours or weeks ago, when I would have been writing this fortified by a glass of white wine at my elbow. I would have justified it by imagining that it stimulated the creative juices, but I must admit there was never any evidence of that.

At this moment, I am writing with a tall glass of sparkling mineral water — chilled and topped with a slice of lemon — as a sort of substitute at hand.

There is, of course, no question of it stimulating the creative juices, or anything else, for that matter. It is, rather, a kind of compensation.

In a remarkably short time, I have become quite familiar with those refreshing bottled waters which have grown in popularity as, increasingly, public water supplies are routinely "doctored". These spring waters festoon the shelves of any supermarket these days, although advertising forbids me to mention them by name.

My preference is for the bubbly, carbonated kind, as opposed to the still variety. From France, I often sample the most vaunted and maybe the priciest of them all. From Ireland, I have tasted one from a source said to be 800 years old. From England, I have shared Her Majesty's enjoyment of probably the best of British — so beloved of Princess Margaret, too, if only in her whisky.

And last, but not least, a couple from deep in the soil of Scotland, and earning, I am happy to say, their fair share of a huge market.

I am wistful, watching the bubbles in my water rising slowly to the rim and feeling somewhat self-righteous. And I would change it, at the drop of a hat, for a glass of dry white wine.

Oh for the buttery, toasted tinge of an Australian Chardonnay or of an exquisite Chablis. Or the grassy, gooseberry flavour of a sip of Sancerre. Not for the first time, I am in total sympathy with Keats, this time in his longing for:

A beaker full of the warm South
full of the true, the blushful Hippocrene,
with beaded bubbles winking at the brim,
and purple-stained mouth.

Unlike the poet, though, I do not enjoy red wine, for the simple reason that I am allergic to it. Correction — "intolerant" is the current medical term to describe what we used to call an allergy but, either way, that is the reaction I have to it.

For heaven's sake, I digress. I still have not explained why I have by my elbow a large tumbler full of pure, spring water instead of a modest glass of crisp, white wine.

After all that, anyone would think I have signed the pledge. I have not. I am merely trying to change the habits of a lifetime. The eating habits, that is.

So am I going on a slimming course? No I am not. What I am doing is trying to switch from some of the foods — quick food, convenience food, fatty food (resorted to in a busy, working life) — to a better regimen.

It is nine years since I lit my last cigarette, but was it worth it, I wonder? I seem to have swopped one bad habit for another. Life, since then, appears to have been a series of diets.

Each one is fine for a while, then it becomes repetitive, boring and ultimately useless. High fibre, low fibre, banana, grapefruit — you name it, I have done it. Inevitably, the scales creep up and in no time I am back to where I started.

What happened after I stopped smoking is not unusual. I put on weight. You give up nicotine and your senses of smell and taste are reinvigorated. Food tastes better so, unconsciously, you take more of it. Psychologists maintain that eating can be compensation for the loss of smoking, but that piece of information does not change a thing.

"Don't keep on buying clothes a size bigger," one experienced friend cautioned. "All you do is keep on filling them."

I do have a weight problem and, although I am not on a diet, as such, one aim is to lose some pounds while, at the same time, developing a routine of healthier eating.

Basically, I suppose, this means less fat, fewer dairy products and less sugar. But it is too soon to tell if it is working or not.

As far as losing weight is concerned, it is, of course, all down to calories. If you take more of them in than you burn up in a day, a week, a month, or a year, you lay down the surplus in fat.

Most drinks, alcoholic or otherwise, also contain some calories, so these must be part of the arithmetic — which explains my glass of spring water.

I should know, for I have tried several slimming regimes before. I am well aware of what to eat and what to avoid but, such is my self-indulgence, that does not seem to help.

And, oddly, it is not the actual dieting I find so hard; it is keeping the weight off after having lost it.

It called for a change of tack, so this time I opted for an approach which is different and which should, in the long run, keep the preferred weight steady, if ever I reach it.

The run up to Diet-Day, however, was the same as ever. As I psyched myself for dreaded deprivation, I went into squirrel mode, eating and drinking enough to lay down for the lean days ahead.

"You won't get that again for a long time," I tell myself, justifying yet another helping of this or that while pouring another glass of my best dry Sancerre. And when, at last, D-Day arrives, I have bumps in all the wrong places.

It is all quite ironic. Many years ago, I supervised, with a qualified dietician, a couple of slimming courses for readers of the Press and Journal and Evening Express. The objective was to prove that milk was not fattening, and we invited readers to go on a week's slimming holiday and put the milk diet to the test.

If I remember rightly, all 10 slimmers on the two courses lost weight. I did not join them on the diet on either occasion because, in those days, I was a quite trim 10 stone, but they will never know how much I sympathised with their hunger pangs and their valiant efforts to stick to the routine.

That was 20 years ago and more so, not surprisingly, I have lost touch with most of them and I wonder often if their experiment of long ago has helped them subsequently to keep their weight in check.

Those who were chosen for one of the courses at a hotel at Banchory in 1971 were: Mrs Joan Gamblin, a doctor's wife from Aberdeen, (now in Inverness); Mrs Evelyn Stewart, wife of a Lossiemouth fisherman; Mrs Thelma Simons, Caithness; Miss Mary Auchnie, Rothienorman; Mrs Jean Garrison, Aberdeen, and Mrs Norma Gerrard, from Skene.

One of the tips they were given then was to exercise, to play, to read, to concentrate on anything to keep the mind off food and everything associated with it.

Oh dear, I knew I should have written about something else. I must go now and pour myself a little Sancerre.

I really must.

February 6, 1993

● *Since this piece appeared, I have had a letter from Mrs Norma Gerrard, who now lives at Inverurie. She wrote: "When I was one of the lucky ones to go on the slimming course, I did not realise it would be a new beginning for me. Over the years, I have gone up and down in weight like a yo-yo. I am at present just over 10 stones, which, for me, now a grandma, isn't too worrying. This is really to say a belated and long-overdue thank-you for that very important start you gave me."*

TOP GEAR

ANYONE with eyes to see cannot fail to have noticed how tartan has taken off as a fashion these days. A prestigious exhibition has been running in New York showing — among other things — how this century's top designers have used it in haute couture.

To me, this is much less interesting than the explosion of popularity of the kilt among men of all ages as a dress for more-formal occasions such as dinners, dances, ceilidhs, and so on. Chaps who wouldn't have been seen dead in it a few years ago now sally forth in it, dressed to the hilt. And a good thing, too.

This was brought home to me personally a week or two ago at a family wedding, where there were more kilts, more tartans than I had ever seen assembled at an event of the kind — not, mind you, that I'm at a wedding every day.

But why, a few of us wondered, the sudden cachet of the kilt? Well, men's clothes, particularly among the young, have become steadily more colourful in recent years. And, we agreed, there isn't a dress in the whole, wide world that makes a man look more splendid, more manly, than the full Highland rig.

More to it than that? We felt there must be. Wishful thinking, perhaps, but we concluded that it had to be an expression of growing national confidence. Maybe it was even a political statement. If it isn't, and the current craze for the kilt turns out to be nothing more than a fashionable fad, a mere fancy dress, then some are going to be left with an expensive little tartan number hanging uselessly at the back of the wardrobe.

But not many, I suspect. The fact is that full Highland dress is costly. There isn't apparently, a whole lot of change out of £500 for the kilt, jacket, waistcoat and shoes alone, never mind accessories such as sporran and skean dhu. So often it makes sense to hire and a lot of credit must go to the dress-hire people for making this marvellous Scottish dress more available; for encouraging its wear and for helping to instruct as to how it should be worn.

Clearly, though, they cannot stock anything but a token selection of the 1,980 registered Scottish tartans, but only a few of the more common ones — and this is where a problem crops up.

"No, we haven't got your tartan among our hire kilts," one dress-hire man was heard to tell a customer, "but we have got this other one and nobody but an expert would know the difference."

Oh, dear. What the man didn't know — or if he knew, he didn't care — is that there is a great deal of etiquette and form of manners attached to wearing the tartan and, if the unwritten rules are to be followed, the worst gaffe a man can make is to wear a tartan to which he is not entitled. It's done all the time, of course, but that doesn't make it correct.

Even I knew that before I did my homework, a self-imposed exercise after failing to identify more than a handful of tartans at the aforementioned wedding. I didn't know, though, that if, like me, you're entitled to more than one tartan (representing different branches of the same clan or family), the worst mistake of all is to wear different ones. You should, apparently, select the tartan of one branch and stick to it.

All this, of course, might be just so much hogwash to some Scots, grown used to having their clothes "pinched" by Americans, Canadians and any Tom, Dick or Harry. To others, including me, the tartan is a personal and evocative thing, symbolic of long roots and brave deeds, a meaningful manifestation of a proud heritage. So strong are feelings about this that some clans and families have restricted their tartans to the use only of those who have a right to wear them.

The irony is that it is usually quite unnecessary for a Scot to purloin somebody else's tartan, because every true Scot is entitled, one way or another, to his own.

If he cannot make the claim through name or ancestry, he can turn to one of several that any Scot can wear. The Hunting Stewart, designed specifically for anyone in this position, is perhaps the best example, but others include the Jacobite, the Culloden or the Caledonia. Or he could wear one of the district tartans, according to where he lives. This category includes the Arran, Roxburgh, Gordon and — would you believe it? — the Aberdeen.

Having said all that, if there is still any doubt about which tartan, and you want to get it right, the thing to do is to write either to The Scottish Tartans Society, Drummond Street, Comrie, Perthshire PH5 2DW, or the the Scots Ancestry Research Society, 3 Albany Street, Edinburgh EH1 3PY. Either, for a fee, will be willing to help.

By the way, although the oldest tartan dates from before 250AD, there is little evidence to support the popular notion that the Jacobites at Culloden were dressed in their respective clan tartans. Groups of soldiers might have worn identical tartan, but this does not necessarily mean that names had been given to the various patterns.

The tartans of today, seemingly, did not get their names until the late 18th Century, and not until the early 19th Century did they become established. At the very least, they should be worn with pride and dignity and respect. In the words of General Sir Colin Campbell at the relief of Lucknow: "Bring forrit that tartan."

That is the motto of the Scottish Tartans Society — and an appropriate one it is.

November 12, 1988

● *A complete kilt outfit may have been obtained for £500 at the time of writing. It would cost , I understand, a great deal more than that now.*

Mrs Mopps

A WORRYING thought occurred to me today. It is that I am probably in danger of becoming addicted — not to booze or drugs or anything so dramatic. The dread thought crossed my mind that I might just be getting hooked on housework.

And what brought this on? Well, I had spent the first couple of hours of the day doing out the ground floor (which left only two rooms to do). Mind you, I had done it thoroughly. Paintwork scrubbed, furniture polished, brasses burnished — the lot. Then I sank into an armchair with a welcome cuppa and switched on the telly. Now that is unusual in itself; not the armchair or the cuppa but the telly. To my certain knowledge, I have never watched TV in the morning.

On the other hand, bored and restless and confined to the house with flu, I must admit looking in sometimes in the afternoons. But I must be just about the only person in the entire country who has never seen breakfast TV.

Out of curiosity, I have even sampled the murky mixture of what passes for programmes in the early hours. Never seen The Hit Man and Her? You're missing nothing. Or James Whale, whose aspiration is to excel himself in his rudeness to his inane phone-in guests? Strictly for morons, I would say.

But why I turned on the box this morning, I cannot say because I do not know. Enough that no sooner had I settled down than I began to feel uneasy, restless … and, yes, guilty.

Which is most unusual because, in truth, I am not given to feeling guilty about very much; and certainly not about anything as innocuous as watching TV or reading or walking my dogs or anything else I happen to enjoy. In fact, I sometimes think I ought to feel guilty when I don't about some of the things I do — or don't do.

It was not as if, this morning, there was a chore crying out to be done. Whatever needed doing could equally well be done, like this column, in the afternoon, or tomorrow, or the day after that. Except, perhaps, the two remaining rooms ...?

In any case, I have come round to the idea that it was not watching the telly that did it but the time I chose to watch it. What? Gawping at the box in the middle of the morning? That is not quite how my old granny would have put it, but that is what she would have meant all the same.

She did not have a degree, my granny — except from the clichéd University of Life — but, if she had been alive today, she would indubitably be one of those clever women who hold down top jobs and manage house and home equally well. I wish I had listened to her more.

With an ease which seemed effortless, she could budget like a banker; run up a pair of curtains while the cake was baking; cook a pheasant Cordon Bleu, having plucked and cleaned it and divined its vintage by an examination of its feathers.

Her house was bright and warm and welcoming, and it shone like a new pin. Friends and family sought its sanctuary in times of celebration and sorrow alike; its ordered tenor exuding a kind of cosy security, a bulwark against the outside world.

In addition, she found time to help to run a business and, in between, had somehow managed to read most of the classics. To think that I was not remotely impressed!

"But I don't want to do housework when I grow up," I would protest innocently as, flitting after her with a duster, I pretended to help.

"Maybe not," she would reply kindly, "but you must know how to do it yourself before asking someone else to do it for you."

I think she understood, though, because housework and housekeeping — to which she brought all the skills of a top-flight manager — were not the be-all and end-all of her own life. In any case, her words have echoed down the years.

Mainly because of a full-time job, I have been in a position, for most of my working life, of having to engage someone else to clean for me. Which is just as well, because I must admit I am not the world's greatest housewife. To me, housework remains a chore — and a boring and repetitive chore at that.

Even so, it must be done. There have been times, though, when I have envied the casual attitude of a friend of long ago.

She was an art student, very personable and likeable, but so unworldly that she would blast out Beethoven on her hi-fi (or whatever it was) or paint a portrait quite oblivious to the half-eaten cat food, dripping dishes, next week's washing and last week's grime.

"Never mind, I'll do it all tomorrow," she would laugh, closing the door on the chaos as she set off for an evening out. We lost touch years ago, but I can only hope that she, too, was in a position to employ someone to do her house.

She was the antithesis, dear soul, of another of my quite eccentric friends who tends still to phone for a chat at the end of the day.

"Phew, I'm all in," she will say, sipping a gin and tonic.

"Why?" I respond obligingly, knowing the reason full well.

"Been at it all day. All over the house. Had to be done — you see, my cleaning lady comes tomorrow."

My cleaning lady left to have a baby not long after I gave up full-time work. Since then, I have been doing my own cleaning.

"Nothing to it," I exclaimed at the time, remembering my much-loved granny.

Well, now I know better. The first thing I have learned is to keep on top of it — which is why, I suppose, I am getting hooked on housework. The other is that, although I detest cleaning, I loathe chaos more.

Now, I must dash. There are still two rooms to be done. And I have read hardly any of the classics.

March 3, 1990

Beware the Ides

TOMORROW is the first day of the month of the wild winds, the mad hares and, tradition has it, if it comes in like a lion, it will go out like a lamb. March is also the month of the Ides. "Beware the Ides of March" — the soothsayer's warning to Cæsar in the great play of that name can still arouse a frisson of foreboding

Shakespeare, interestingly, had based it all on fact. Cæsar was assassinated on the Ides of March and, according to Plutarch, many people reported a soothsayer forewarning him of great danger threatening him at that time.

That day, on his way to the Senate House, Cæsar called out to the soothsayer: "The Ides of March have come" – to which the soothsayer answered softly: "Yes, but they are not yet gone."

So what are the Ides? They are, in the old Roman calendar, the 15th of March and the 15th of May, July and October, and they are the 13th of any other month. But they were not, traditionally, intrinsically unlucky, not in the way that the 13th is. Especially Friday the 13th which, as it happens, is only 13 days away.

I must say that I will not be taking any particular care that day because the 13th and the number 13 have always been quite lucky for me. Not that I am particularly superstitious. At least, I do not think that I am.

However, I am loath, for one thing, to turn back after setting out on a journey. Only the other day, I would not return to the house to pick up the gloves I had left lying on the table.

Turning back would bring misfortune, my old granny used to say. "Wait there! Don't turn back," she would call as, retreating, she would herself fetch the forgotten object. I wonder what I would do if I found I had left something crucial behind, such as flight tickets or even a passport? Of course, I would have to return and collect them. But I would not do so easily.

From my early days, I have not inherited a large legacy of superstition as some people have. One or two do persist, however, such as the colour green. For reasons never quite explained, it was not a shade to be chosen lightly, or even at all. It did not bring good fortune.

Years later, I fancied the darkest of dark green as the finish for a new car. I hesitated and dithered, remembering the superstition, but in the end decided to have it. British Racing Green it was called, if I remember rightly, but what is more important, the car turned out to be one of the best I have had. Green, since then, has held no bad vibes for me.

It was from school friends that I learned a lot about North-east superstitious lore. Some of them belonged to that brave breed of stoic folk, fishing people who live in tightly knit communities around our North-east coast. Close to the elements, never far from life and death, they are among the most superstitious people on earth.

Once, walking home with a school friend from the cinema, she told me something which has stayed in my memory. The night was very dark and the stars hung like lanterns, almost close enough to touch. Suddenly, there was the faint flash of a shooting star.

Shivering, she clutched my arm. "Someone has just died," she whispered, "and that was the angel coming down to fetch the soul."

She also told me that seagulls are really the souls of drowned seafarers given new life. So it was unlucky to kill a gull. If one of them flew against a window, that was a sign of danger for one of the family at sea. And if, on the other hand, seamen saw three of them flying together, that was taken as an omen of death.

Since then, I have become familiar with lots of lore and legends about birds. There are magpies in my garden but, if I see one, I tend to look around for his mate:

> *One for sorrow, two for mirth,*
> *Three for a wedding, four for a birth,*
> *Five for silver, six for gold,*
> *Seven for a secret not to be told.*

The raven is said to be a bird of ill-fortune. To hear a raven croak before you set out on a journey is believed to be very bad luck. In the Highlands, on the other hand, deerstalkers were convinced that hearing a raven croak before they set out brought very good fortune.

Then there is the legend about the tame ravens which live at the Tower of London. If they ever depart for good – so the well-known story goes – the Crown will fall and Britain with it.

There is, though, more to superstition than simply carrying a lucky mascot or avoiding walking under a ladder. It is often triggered off when someone is anxious or afraid of a situation thought to be beyond control.

Is it apprehension before setting out on a fishing trip; is it fear of going down to the depths in little ships that sparks off some of the beliefs of our God-fearing fishermen? That it is unlucky to meet a cat or a minister before going on board; that it is unlucky to set sail on a Sunday (or lucky, depending on where you come from); that it is not good to whistle at sea for fear of summoning up a storm?

One of my recent ploys has been to fashion a little woodland walk out of a piece of waste ground. My planting plan featured more than one rowan simply because the mountain ash is indigenous and, in any case, I like it.

I was not aware that its presence in many a country garden was thought to ward off evil spirits. I did not know – but what a bonus!

February 29, 1992

END OF THE LINE

IF I HAD only taken the trouble to listen more carefully to my grandfather, John Murray, I would have learned a lot and gathered enough material for a book. In nostalgic mood, he would reminisce about his boyhood in Upper Banffshire, on a wee place in the Cabrach.

From earliest days, I have been familiar with that barren but bonnie landscape dominated by a heathery hill called The Buck. It was there that my grandfather and his brothers hunted the white mountain hares; learned how to bring down a grouse, and how to land a fish from a gurgling burn.

On frequent visits, I never cease to marvel how anyone dependent on the land for a living could scratch even the most meagre subsistence—let alone make enough to rear a large family.

My grandfather was one of 12, sons and daughters born to strict, but loving, parents around the end of last century, one of the youngest of whom was Auntie Cath, my great-aunt, who was born a year before the Queen Mother.

Theirs was a happy home and, in the closeness of their large circle, they learned how to get along with each other and, therefore, how to get on with other folk.

As far as I know, they grew up, every one of them, to acquit themselves well although, naturally, some did better in a material sense than others. Which matters not in the least for, as far as I am concerned, money and the amassing of it is a poor measure of a man's true worth.

In any case, they grew into a hardy breed, fairly typical, I would imagine, of our auld Scots folk — a breed, alas, which has all but vanished. They were hard-working, God-fearing, respected and fiercely independent — and, it is sometimes whispered, as thrawn as Auld Nick himself.

My ancestors are, to me, rather sketchy, shadowy figures of whom I know only a little; mere bits and pieces about them, not enough to tell what they were really like as individuals.

Of that doughty dozen, Alex, a bright-eyed laddie, went soldiering in World War I and fought in that hell which was The Somme. Did he, in dying, hear the call of the curlew on The Buck, see again the white hare bounding through the heather? In those last moments, did his thoughts turn briefly in the muck and the mud to the old folk at home? Sorely, they grieved for him.

Alex Murray died gallantly on the field of battle, but his young body did not come home to rest with his ancestors on the green sward around the roofless ruin of the Auld Kirk at Auchindoir. His is an unknown grave, somewhere in France.

I have often dallied there, at Auchindoir, where long-gone generations slumber side by side under flat stone tablets which proffer the occasional clue.

"They lived and died in the land of Craig", one inscription pronounces on one blessed pair. Did they tarry for a lifetime from choice, or did circumstances leave no alternative? The former, I like to think, for the epitaph has a contented ring.

Nearby, another proclaims that she who rests below was a missionary in China. Why, in His wisdom, the Good Lord chose a lassie from this douce backwater to do His work in a faraway land is anybody's guess.

At any rate, the large family left their mute forefathers behind and moved up country to a bigger place in the valley at Glass, near Huntly. There they remained until all, save one, had gone their separate ways.

Ellen must have felt desolate as she watched her old home fall under the auctioneer's hammer, and she planned to make her home with a married sister. Little did she know that in that ending there was, for her, a beginning. In six months, she had married the lad who, that day, gave her a lift to her sister's house on the pillion of his motorbike.

Last Saturday, with a lingering sadness, we drove to the old kirk at Glass on a lovely autumn day which had in it the first signs of the year's ending. Our mission was to bid a final farewell; to pay our last respects to Auntie Cath, the last of her brave line.

Thirty-four years ago, to the very day, she had watched in that same church as her only daughter, Hazel, wed the man of her choice. From that happy union, she was given, in the fullness of time, a grandson, who brought her pleasure, especially when he graduated in law from Aberdeen University a few years ago.

To mourn too much seemed inappropriate, and thankfulness was more in order, for she had enjoyed a very long and fulfilled life surrounded, to the end, by her nearest and dearest.

In the sunshine, she was laid to rest with the husband she lost 10 years before.

At moments like these, we are confronted by our own mortality and, standing in that peaceful country kirkyard, we talked about the early hairst and the tattie crop ... drawing comfort from things ordinary, yet eternal.

And so we repaired for tea, taking solace from each other's company, bound mostly by ties of blood which, in the end, are maybe the strongest ties of all, meeting again some of the clan we tend to see only at weddings and funerals — even one or two who, to mutual shame, we had not met before.

Sad, we were, on the way home, naturally, for it is particularly poignant when goes the last of the line; the last of a generation. It is the end of an era; the breaking of a cherished link.

I wish I had known better my great aunt and her siblings. I wish I had listened carefully to my grandfather. They could have told me so much more about their lives and times and about their remarkable family.

The paramount emotion on the drive back was not sadness. It was a sense of pride ... that the blood which ran so true in their veins runs also in mine.

September 15, 1990